Edited by Jim Heimann with
an introduction by Willy Wilkerson

The Golden Age of Advertising – the 60s

TASCHEN

KÖLN LONDON LOS ANGELES MADRID PARIS TOKYO

Steven Heller:

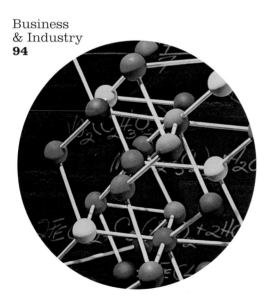

RICAN

Advertising in the Sixties:

So, What's the Big Idea?

by Steven Heller

If the advertisements in this volume were the sole artifacts a historian used to examine and analyze the turbulent Sixties, a picture of American culture would emerge that bears scant resemblance to social and political realities of the times. Where are the Blacks, Latinos, or Asians? Viewed from this vantage point, the Sixties had no civil rights protest, Vietnam War, or sex, drugs, and rock and roll—at least not in any meaningful way. The advertisements here, exhumed from the crypts of Madison Avenue as mummified in the mass magazines of the day, were sanitized, homogenized, and cauterized, which is not to say that they did not have style, taste, or humor, or that they do not represent the zeitgeist in a jaundiced way.

Advertising is, after all, artificial truth. Of course, certain claims are accurate—makeup hides blemishes, soda is sweet, bad breath smells, headaches hurt, and sunglasses shade the eyes. Definitely, by the Sixties, phony snake oil and patent medicine advertisements from the turn of the century were long since abolished. Yet advertising, especially at this time, was nonetheless designed to out-smart, out-do, and out-sell

competition no matter what it was, through whatever means was tolerable within the parameters of so-called "truth in advertising" doctrines—which is a concept akin to allowing acceptable amounts of rat hair in food. Fabrications and exaggerations existed but no one cared because the images, words, and concepts toed the line between the possible and the preposterous. What's more, by the early Sixties post-war Americans were happily conditioned to believe anything that mass media put forth, and advertising was embraced without question or hesitation. Consequently, many magazine ads and TV commercials were viewed more as entertainment—or pastimes—than as crass sales pitches.

During the Sixties, advertising evolved from its primordial emphasis on lengthy, turgid texts to snappy, witty headline and picture ensembles through a method known as the "Big Idea". The term connotes both a radical shift from the past and a distinctly American genre of creative promotion. The pioneers of the so-called "Creative Revolution", out of which the Big Idea emerged, realized that to truly capture an audience's attention and impart lasting messages they had to continually amuse. So to keep the public on their feet Mad Ave had to call in some of its biggest creative guns.

The gun is an apt metaphor because an advertising campaign is no different from a battlefield maneuver. The larger the artillery or the better the strategy or the greater the manpower, the more hearts and minds will be won over. Continual bombardment of slogans and images clearly reduced resistance and built recognition. If the product being advertised actually lived up to the claims, so much the better. But this was not even necessary if the battle was uncontested. Witness the advertisements for some of the Sixties' leading brands—Maidenform®, Anacin®, General Electric, and Clairol. While the products efficiently did their jobs, in each case their manufactured auras and fake mythologies gave them stature and sales appeal so that each commanded a strong

market share, until eventually they were challenged by an even more formidable mythologizing force. Fortunes of existing products were often changed through smarter, if also more relentless, advertising campaigns, and new brands earned affluence through what in the Madison Avenue argot is known as spectacular "creative".

Witness the Sixties campaign for Volkswagen created by Doyle Dane Bernbach that took a little Nazi "people's" car designed in the late 1930s under Adolf Hitler's auspices and instantly made it the best selling economy car in big-car-loving America by claiming its perceived deficits were truly advantages. That was strategic ingenuity and brilliant advertising. Or take the ad for the portable Sony, a tiny TV made in Japan (another former wartime adversary), home of the cheap transistor radio, which, through witty copy and image, propelled the brand into direct competition with American-made giants.

During the Sixties, the Big Idea made advertising decidedly cleverer, funnier, and more enjoyable than ever before. New standards were set by the wunderkinder of Madison Avenue, such as art directors George Lois, Gene Federico, Bill Taubin, Helmut

Krone, Bob Gage, and others who captured the power inherent in good typography and strong imagery to add touches of class to ads that did not turn noses up at the masses but afforded them greater respect. Yet their respective gems were set alongside many cheaper stones. The Sixties was a transitory period in which the Creative Revolution fought the mediocre status quo. And mediocre does not imply unprofessional, either. A typical ad for Swift Premium breakfast sausage—which uses a photograph that imitates a Norman Rockwell painting replete with Betty Crocker® mom and two clean-cut varsity brothers good-naturedly fighting over the machine-processed delicacy—cost considerable money and energy to produce. Yet the creators apparently lacked the vision and intuition that an exemplary ad, even for such a quotidian product as pork sausage, could use wit to transcend cliché. Similarly, despite the idiotic simplicity of an early Sixties ad for the soft drink, Dr Pepper, which sought to siphon market share away from Coke® and Pepsi®, and shows a thirsty lass dreaming of another Pepper, was a costly exercise for the advertising agency. Just getting the model's

mouth, eyes, and hair perfect enough to seduce someone into drinking a beverage with Pepper (not to mention Doctor) in the name took considerable hubris. Yet an ad for 7 UP®, which had as much to gain from tried-and-true advertisements as Dr Pepper, used a much more unconventional expressive approach: Rather than a photograph or realistic painting, the bold step of using a conceptual illustration of a man watching a football game (seen in the lens of his binoculars), with barely a hint of the bottle (it was convention in all such ads to show the product), gave the viewer an added message to ponder. Now that was gutsy. Slowly mass market advertisements were injected with more original attributes.

However, Sixties advertising inherited Fifties hold-overs that worked so well during the Age of Eisenhower there was no need to change in the Age of Camelot. Budweiser's® "Where There's Life There's Bud" campaign continued for almost a generation with little modification. The picture-perfect paintings of sultry dames or smooth playboys with tall glasses of foamy brew poured before their eyes was so ingrained in the vernacular that MAD magazine, infamous for its parody

advertisements, did a send-up featuring a woeful drunk under the title "Not Happier But Wiser". Despite this critical implication, having a slogan, jingle, or logo so indelibly a part of American language was free advertising.

The Sixties gave birth to its own classics rooted in crafty headlines and taglines designed to wheedle into the mass subconscious. Many were innocuous, others insipid. Of the latter, cigarettes slogans were often the most memorable, including one for Lucky Strike Filters that went "Show Me A Filter Cigarette That Really Delivers and I'll Eat My Hat!" While the verbiage may seem unwieldy, it was unforgettable when wed to a photograph of an attractive model whose hat has a large bite chomped out it. One ad in this lengthy campaign apparently shows a Vietnamese woman sheepishly smiling under her traditional straw headgear in perhaps one of the few tips of the hat, so to speak, to America's geo-political involvement in Southeast Asia (as a dumping ground for cigarettes, among other things). Another monumental ad of the day and thematic constant in American vernacular was

the "Be Sociable, Have a Pepsi" campaign. Most of the ads included photo-realistic paintings of young middle class "Sociables" who "prefer Pepsi" cavorting at the ski lounge and penthouses of America. The ad not only encouraged its target audience to live life with gusto, the slogan was a mantra for a generation.

Certain advertisements are considered classics because they somehow promoted a lifestyle that became an integral part of the zeitgeist. Clairol's ads, for example, made it socially imperative for every woman to change their hair color, and the slogan "Does She Or Doesn't She, Only Her Hairdresser Knows for Sure," underscored how easy and effective it was. Yet others are classic because they actually changed the way the public viewed their surroundings. Braniff International airline's "The End of the Plain Plane, Explained" introduced an old product with a new aura. In fact, the product itself was a veritable billboard. To make an otherwise small Portuguese air carrier appeal to a large segment of American air travelers, the color of the planes themselves were changed from the usual metallic silver to various primary and pastel

hues. The change had little to do with improved service, but nonetheless signaled a perceived revolution in the air and on the ground, with the idea that an airline was not merely an impersonal, utilitarian conveyor but an exciting (colorful) experience.

Advertising will never be neutral. It must always demonstrate that one thing is better than the next thing, and that that thing is also the best thing. During the Sixties the definition of hard-sell changed from bang-the-consumer-over-the-head with trite words and pictures to creative playfulness presumably geared to make the receiver feel better about advertising. And it worked. But regardless of method the advertisements in this volume—truly the backbone of a market-driven capitalist economy—are driven by one simple agenda: To build such incomparable recognition that the public will clamor for, desire, and demand whatever is being sold to them. And that in a nutshell is the Big Idea.

Steven Heller is the author and editor of over 80 books on graphic design and popular culture, including *Design Literacy: Understanding Graphic Design*, *The Graphic Design Reader*, *Graphic Style: From Victorian to Digital*, and *Counter Culture: The Allure of Mini-Mannequins*.

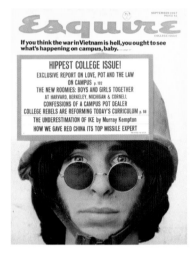

Werben in den Sechzigern:

Auf der Suche nach der „Big Idea"

von Stephen Heller

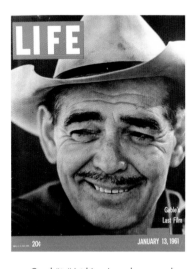

Man stelle sich einmal vor, die Werbeanzeigen in diesem Band wären das einzige Quellenmaterial, auf das sich ein Historiker bei seiner Beschäftigung mit den turbulenten sechziger Jahren stützen könnte. Das Bild, das auf diese Weise von der amerikanischen Gesellschaft entstehen würde, hätte mit der sozialen und politischen Realität jener Zeit nur eine sehr entfernte Ähnlichkeit. Denn: Wo sind die Schwarzen, die Latinos oder Asiaten? In der Werbung nahm man weder die Proteste der Bürgerrechtsbewegung, noch den Vietnamkrieg, noch Sex and Drugs and Rock 'n' Roll zur Kenntnis – oder bestenfalls ganz am Rande. Was sich in den verstaubten Archiven der großen Werbeagenturen an der New Yorker Madison Avenue ausgraben lässt, was sich gleichsam mumifiziert in den Publikumszeitschriften jener Tage erhalten hat, war immer schon lauter. Das heißt jedoch nicht, dass es den Anzeigen an Stil, Geschmack oder Humor gefehlt oder dass sie nicht dem Zeitgeist entsprochen hätten.

Werbung ist letztendlich eine künstlich erzeugte Wahrheit. Manche Behauptungen waren zwar zutreffend – Make-up überdeckt Schönheitsfehler, Limo schmeckt süß,

schlechter Atem riecht übel, Kopfschmerzen tun weh und Sonnenbrillen schützen die Augen vor Sonne – und die zur Jahrhundertwende üblichen Anzeigen für falsches Schlangenöl und Patentmedizin waren in den Sechzigern längst passé. Doch nach wie vor legte es die Werbung darauf an, die Konkurrenz auszustechen und auszutricksen – und zwar auf allen Gebieten und mit allen Mitteln, die nach dem „Truth-in-Advertising"-Gesetz, einem Gesetz gegen den irreführenden und unlauteren Wettbewerb, gerade noch zulässig waren. Und das waren viele. Auf anderem Gebiet wären die Bestimmungen etwa der Vorschrift gleichgekommen, die zulässige Höchstmenge für Rattenhaar in Lebensmitteln nicht zu überschreiten. Es wurde übertrieben und vorgegaukelt, was jedoch niemanden störte, weil die Bilder, Worte und Konzepte ohnehin im Grenzbereich von Sinnigem und Widersinnigem angesiedelt waren. Außerdem waren die Amerikaner in den frühen Sechzigern schon so erfolgreich darauf getrimmt, alles zu glauben, was die Massenmedien verkündeten, dass sie auch die Werbung unkritisch und bedenkenlos konsumierten. Folglich wurden Zeitschriftenanzeigen und Fernsehspots eher als Unterhaltung betrachtet denn als reine Verkaufsmasche.

In den Sechzigern entwickelte sich die Werbung weg von langen Texten hin zu bildorientierten Kompositionen mit spritzigen Headlines. Ganz so, wie es das „Big-Idea"-Konzept forderte. Die Suche nach der zentralen Werbeidee, dem zündenden Funken zur Vermarktung eines Produkts, bedeutete eine radikale Abkehr von den Strategien der Vergangenheit und führte zu einem originär amerikanischen Genre der kreativen Werbung. Die Pioniere der „Creative Revolution", aus der die „Big Idea" hervorging, hatten nämlich entdeckt, dass sie ihr Publikum immer wieder von neuem unterhalten mussten, um seine Aufmerksamkeit zu fesseln und Aussagen nachhaltiger vermitteln zu können. Wenn die Madison Ave ihre Zielgruppen also bei der Stange halten wollte, musste sie schweres kreatives Geschütz auffahren.

„Geschütz" ist hier eine sehr passende Metapher, weil sich eine Werbekampagne in nichts von einem militärischen Feldzug unterscheidet: Je schlagkräftiger die Artillerie, je besser die Strategie oder je größer die Truppenstärke, desto mehr Herzen und Sympathien lassen sich erobern. Ein anhaltendes Bombardement mit Slogans und Bildern zermürbt spürbar die Widerstandskraft und erhöht den Wiedererkennungsgrad. Wenn dann das beworbene Produkt den behaupteten Eigenschaften auch entsprach, war das natürlich umso besser. Unbedingt notwendig war es nicht. Denn nicht immer gab es echte Gegner – genannt seien hier die Kampagnen für einige der in den sechziger Jahren führenden Marken: Maidenform®, Anacin®, General Electric und Clairol. Die Produkte erfüllten nicht nur einfach ihren Zweck. Die um sie kreierte Aura und der geliehene Mythos verliehen ihnen Status und Sales-Appeal. Auf diese Weise hielten sie große Marktanteile. Anders, wenn ein neuer Gegner auftauchte, der sie mit noch gewaltigerer Mythologisierungsmacht herausforderte: Oft wendete sich dann das Geschick etablierter Produkte und neue Marken gewannen Zulauf durch spektakulä-

re „creatives", wie solche smarten Kampagnen im Jargon der Madison Ave genannt werden.

So entwarfen Doyle Dane Bernbach in den Sechzigern für Volkswagen eine Kampagne, die den kleinen, Ende der Dreißiger unter Nazi-Schirmherrschaft konstruierten „Käfer" über Nacht zum bestverkauften Kleinwagen im straßenkreuzerfixierten Amerika machte. Sie stilisierten mögliche Nachteile des „Volkswagens" zu Vorteilen. Das war eine strategisch geniale, eine brillante Werbung. Ähnlich war es mit dem tragbaren Sony-Fernseher, der in Japan (wie Deutschland ein ehemaliger Kriegsgegner der USA und zudem Heimat des billigen Transistorradios) hergestellt wurde: Mit ihrer cleveren Text- und Bildgestaltung katapultierte die Sony-Anzeige das Mini-TV in einen direkten Wettbewerb zu den großen amerikanischen Konkurrenzprodukten.

Infolge des „Big-Idea"-Prinzips war die Werbung in den Sechzigern pfiffiger, lustiger und unterhaltsamer als je zuvor. Die „Wunderkinder" von der Mad Ave – Artdirectors wie George Lois, Gene Federico, Bill Taubin, Helmut Krone, Bob Gage, die die Macht einer guten Typografie und einer intensiven

Bildsprache erkannt hatten – setzten neue Maßstäbe. Mit Raffinesse kreierten sie Anzeigen, die den Bedürfnissen der Masse mehr Respekt zollten und auf eine elitäre Abgrenzung verzichteten. Das waren allerdings nur seltene Glanzlichter im grauen Gesamtszenario, denn die Sechziger waren eine Zeit des Umbruchs, in der die „Creative Revolution" gegen das vorherrschende Mittelmaß anzukämpfen hatte. Und Mittelmaß muss ja auch nicht zwangsläufig Unprofessionalität bedeuten. Eine typische Werbung wie die für Swift Premium Breakfast Sausage setzte beispielsweise auf ein Foto, das einer Illustration von Norman Rockwell nachempfunden war und eine typische Betty-Crocker®-Mama mit zwei adretten Musterknaben zeigte, die sich fröhlich um die Allerweltsdelikatesse balgten. Die Anzeige war recht teuer und aufwändig produziert. Doch ihren Machern fehlte es offenbar an einer Vision und an Intuition, sonst hätten sie erkannt, dass kreative Werbung selbst für ein so alltägliches Produkt wie Würstchen mit etwas Witz herkömmliche Klischees überwinden kann. Auch eine Anzeige für den Softdrink Dr Pepper® aus den frühen Sechzigern war zwar denkbar

simpel gestrickt, kostete die Werbeagentur aber viel Arbeit. Um den Konkurrenten Coke® und Pepsi® das Wasser abzugraben wurde ein Mädel gezeigt, das nach einem zweiten Pepper-Drink dürstete. Mochten Mund, Augen und Haar des Models auch noch so perfekt sein: Schon allein der Versuch, möglichst viele Menschen für ein Getränk mit Namen „Pfeffer" zu begeistern (von dem Namenszusatz „Doktor" ganz zu schweigen), zeugte von größtem Selbstvertrauen. Und obwohl es für 7 UP® ebenso interessant gewesen wäre wie für Dr Peppe sich praxisbewährter Werbemethoden zu bedienen, ging 7 UP® einen wesentlich unkonventionelleren Weg. Anstatt auf eine Fotografie oder ein realistisch gemaltes Bilc zu setzen, wagte man sich einen Schritt vor und zeigte nur schemenhaft einen Mann, der sich ein Football-Spiel anschaut (das sich auf den Gläsern seiner Sonnenbrille widerspiegelte). Ungewöhnlich auch, dass die 7-UP-Flasche bloß angedeutet war, denn konventionelle Anzeigen betonten stets das Produkt. Die ausgefallene Bildsprache gab dem Betrachter zu denken und enthielt eine zusätzliche Botschaft. Ein mutiger Schritt. Nach und nach zeigten sich immer mehr Anzeigenkampagnen von originellen Einfällen inspiriert.

Die Werbung der Sechziger übernahm aber auch Dauerbrenner aus den Fünfzigern, die in der Ära Eisenhower so gut funktioniert hatten, dass gar kein Anlass bestand, sie in der Kennedy-Ära zu ändern. Die Budweiser®-Kampagne „Where There's Life There's Bud" lief mit nur geringfügigen Veränderungen nahezu eine ganze Generation lang weiter. Hohe Gläser, die vor den Augen gepflegter Rasseweiber und smarter Playboys mit schäumendem Gerstensaft gefüllt werden: Dieses Bild war so tief in Alltagskultur und -sprache verwurzelt, dass es die für ihre Werbeparodien berüchtigte Zeitschrift MAD reizte, einen zerknirschten Zecher unter dem Motto „Not Happier But Wiser" zu karikieren. Trotz dieser Stichelei kam es im Grunde natürlich einer kostenlosen Publicity gleich, mit einem Slogan, Jingl

der Logo im amerikanischen Bewusstsein räsent zu sein.

In den Sechzigern entstanden auch echte Klassiker mit raffinierten Headlines und ointen, die darauf abzielten, in das Unterewusstsein der Masse einzudringen. Viele avon waren harmlos und einigen fehlte ogar jeder Pep. Das trifft vor allem auf Werbeslogans für Zigaretten zu, und besonders uf einen für Lucky Strike Filters: „Show Me Filter Cigarette That Really Delivers and ll Eat My Hat!" So schwerfällig der Wortchwall auch daherkommt, er wurde doch nvergesslich durch das dazugehörige Foto ines attraktiven Models mit angebissenem lut. Eine andere Anzeige innerhalb dieser nglebigen Werbekampagne zeigt eine Vietamesin, die verlegen lächelnd unter dem raditionellen Strohhut hervorgrüßt – vielicht eine Anspielung auf das geopolitische ngagement der Vereinigten Staaten, die en südostasiatischen Markt unter anderem uch mit Zigaretten zu Dumping-Preisen berschwemmten. Eine weitere unvergessee Großkampagne rief dazu auf, gesellig zu ein und Pepsi® zu trinken – „Be Sociable, lave a Pepsi". Fast alle Illustrationen zeigen junge Menschen aus der Mittelschicht,

die sich in Amerikas Skilokalen und Penthouses tummeln und offensichtlich gern Pepsi trinken. „Prefer Pepsi" hieß denn auch ein weiterer Slogan. Die Pepsi-Werbung ermutigte, das Leben zu genießen, und die Slogans wurden zu Mantras einer ganzen Generation.

Bestimmte Anzeigen gelten heute als Klassiker, weil sie einen Lifestyle propagierten, der dem Zeitgeist entsprach. So machte die Clairol-Werbung das Haarefärben zur gesellschaftlichen Pflichtübung für jede Frau und unterstrich mit dem Slogan „Does She Or Doesn't She, Only Her Hairdresser Knows", wie einfach und effektiv Färben mit Clairol war. Andere wiederum wurden zu Klassikern, weil sie die Wahrnehmung der Menschen veränderten. Unter dem Motto „The End of the Plain Plane, Explained" präsentierte Braniff International Airways ein altbekanntes Produkt in neuer Hülle. Das Produkt selbst wurde zu einer Werbefläche. Um die eher kleine Fluggesellschaft für möglichst viele Reisende attraktiv zu machen, lackierte man die Flugzeuge in Primär- und Pastellfarben statt in den üblichen Metallic- und Silbertönen. Das hatte nichts mit einem verbesserten Service zu tun, kündigte aber eine Revolution am Himmel und auf Erden an, denn es suggerierte, dass eine Fluggesellschaft nicht nur ein unpersönliches, nützliches Transportunternehmen sein kann, sondern auch aufregende, bunte Abenteuer zu bieten hat.

Werbung wird nie neutral sein. Stets muss sie behaupten, dass eine Sache besser als eine andere ist, und auch diese andere Sache soll selbstredend die Beste sein. In den Sechzigern nahm man Abschied von aggressiven Werbestrategien. Anstatt die Verbraucher mit schalen Phrasen und Bildern zu erschlagen, versuchte man nun mit kreativer Verspieltheit ihre emotionale Einstellung zur Werbung zu verbessern. Und das funktionierte. Ganz unabhängig von den jeweiligen Methoden, mit denen die einzelnen Anzeigen auch in diesem Buch operieren: Als Rückgrat jeder kapitalistischen Marktwirtschaft verfolgt die Werbung natür-

lich ein ganz simples Ziel. Es gilt, einen so hohen Grad der Wiedererkennung zu erreichen, dass die Konsumenten bejubeln, ersehnen und verlangen, was immer man ihnen verkaufen möchte. Und genau das ist – auf einen kurzen Nenner gebracht – die „Big Idea".

Steven Heller ist Autor und Herausgeber von mehr als 80 Büchern über Grafikdesign und Populärkultur, unter anderem von Design Literacy: *Understanding Graphic Design, The Graphic Design Reader, Graphic Style: From Victorian to Digital* und *Counter Culture: The Allure of Mini-Mannequins*.

La publicité des années 60 :

C'est quoi la Grande Idée ?

par Steven Hiller

Si les publicités contenues dans ce volume étaient les uniques sources à la disposition de l'historien pour étudier et analyser les turbulentes années 60, il en émergerait une image de la culture américaine bien éloignée des réalités sociales et politiques de l'époque. Car où sont les Noirs, les Latinos et les Asiatiques ? Vues d'ici, les années 60 n'auraient pas connu les manifestations pour les droits civiques, ni la guerre du Viêtnam, le sexe, la drogue ou le rock'n roll – du moins pas de façon signifiante. Les publicités que l'on voit ici sont exhumées des cryptes de Madison Avenue, telles qu'elles ont été momifiées dans les magazines grand public de ces années-là. Elles sont aseptisées, homogénéisées, cautérisées. Cela ne signifie pas qu'elles soient dépourvues de style, de goût ou d'humour, ni qu'elles ne représentent pas le *zeitgeist*, façon amère.

Après tout, la publicité se fonde sur une vérité artificielle. Bien sûr, certaines affirmations demeurent exactes : le maquillage dissimule les défauts, les sodas sont sucrés, la mauvaise haleine sent, la migraine fait mal et les lunettes de soleil protègent les yeux. A l'évidence, les publicités début de siècle pour fausses huiles de serpent et remèdes de charlatan ont disparu et depuis longtemps. Mais la publicité, alors et plus que jamais, vise à surpasser toute concurrence possible en intelligence, en savoir-faire et en volume de vente, quels que soient les moyens, pourvus qu'ils s'inscrivent dans une doctrine de prétendue « vérité publicitaire » – concept qui reviendrait à admettre la présence d'une quantité acceptable de poils de rat dans notre nourriture. Les falsifications et les exagérations ne manquent pas, mais tout le monde s'en fiche car les images, les mots et les concepts respectent la distinction entre le possible et l'absurde. De plus, au début des années 60, les Américains d'après-guerre sont merveilleusement conditionnés à croire tout ce que racontent les médias, et toute réclame est acceptée sans la moindre remise en question. Par conséquent, les nombreuses publicités de magazines ou de télévision sont davantage considérées comme du divertissement – ou du passe-temps – que comme des boniments accrocheurs.

Au cours de cette période, la publicité passe de textes longs et ampoulés à des ensembles de slogans et d'images incisifs et pleins d'esprit, selon la méthode dite de « la Grande Idée ». Cette expression dénote à la fois un changement radical par rapport au passé, et un genre spécifiquement américain, consistant à promouvoir l'esprit de créativité. Les pionniers de la prétendue « Révolution créative », d'où émerge le concept de la Grande Idée, comprennent que pour capter l'attention du public et imposer des messages durables, il faut amuser, et ceci en permanence. Donc, pour garder le public en éveil, Madison Avenue fait sonner la charge de ses meilleurs créatifs.

Sonner la charge est une bonne métaphore car une campagne publicitaire diffère à peine d'une manœuvre de bataille. Plus la puissance de feu est grande, la stratégie fine et les ressources en hommes abondantes, plus on gagnera les cœurs et les esprits. Un bombardement continu de slogans et d'images réduit manifestement la résistance

et garantit la reconnaissance du produit vanté. Si ce dernier tient réellement ses promesses, tant mieux. Mais cela n'est pas nécessaire, surtout si la bataille est sans adversaire. En témoignent les publicités pour certaines des plus grandes marques de l'époque : Maidenform®, Anacin®, General Electric et Clairol. Tandis que les produits font efficacement leur travail, leur aura fabriquée et leur fausse mythologie confèrent à chacun, une stature et un attrait commercial tels, qu'ils peuvent s'assurer une forte part de marché, jusqu'au moment où ils en viennent à être contestés par une puissance mythologique plus formidable encore. Le sort de produits existants est souvent modifié par des campagnes publicitaires plus astucieuses, mais aussi plus acharnées, tandis que de nouvelles marques prospèrent grâce à ce que l'argot de Madison Avenue appellera du « créatif » spectaculaire.

Ainsi, dans les années 60, la campagne publicitaire lancée pour Volkswagen par Doyle Dane Bernbach, fait d'une petite voiture nazie, conçue « pour le peuple », vers la fin des années 30 et sous les auspices d'Adolf Hitler, la voiture économique la

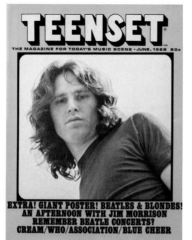

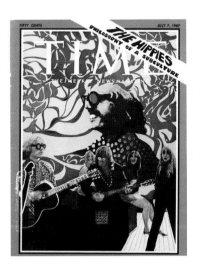

mieux vendue, dans une Amérique habituée aux grosses cylindrées, en affirmant que ses défauts évidents sont en fait de réels avantages. C'est le meilleur exemple d'ingéniosité stratégique et de génie publicitaire. De même, la campagne pour la Sony portative, minuscule télévision fabriquée au Japon (autre ancien ennemi de guerre), roi du transistor bon marché, qui propulse la marque, face à la concurrence directe avec les géants d'origine américaine, et grâce à des slogans et des images pleins d'esprit.

De toute évidence, ces années-là, la Grande Idée rend la publicité plus intelligente, plus drôle et plus divertissante que jamais. De nouvelles règles sont fixées par les enfants prodiges de Madison Avenue, tels les directeurs artistiques George Lois, Gene Federico, Bill Taubin, Helmut Krone ou Bob Gage. Tous s'ingénient à capturer la force inhérente à une bonne typographie et à une imagerie forte, pour donner une certaine classe à des publicités qui, loin de mépriser les masses, leur accordent le plus grand des respects. Pourtant, leurs joyaux respectifs côtoient souvent des bijoux de pacotille. Les années 60 sont une période de transition au cours de laquelle la Révo-

lution créative s'attaque à la médiocrité en place. Or, là encore, médiocrité ne signifie pas manque de professionnalisme. Une publicité typique vantant la saucisse à petit-déjeuner Swift Premium – avec une photographie imitant un tableau de Norman Rockwell qui montre une maman façon Betty Crocker® et deux frères bon chic étudiant, en train de se chamailler gentiment pour cette gâterie industrielle – coûte beaucoup d'argent et beaucoup d'énergie. Pourtant ses créateurs n'ont apparemment ni la vision, ni l'intuition que ce genre de publicité, même pour un produit aussi courant que de la saucisse de porc, pourrait introduire une pointe d'humour, afin de dépasser le cliché. De même, et malgré sa simplicité désarmante, la publicité pour Dr Pepper (Poivre), boisson sans alcool, dont l'objectif déclaré est de siphonner des parts de marché à Coca-Cola® et Pepsi®, et qui montre une jeune fille assoiffée rêvant d'une deuxième bouteille de Pepper, est une affaire coûteuse pour son agence. Il faut rendre les lèvres, les yeux et les cheveux du mannequin assez attrayants pour donner envie d'une boisson dont le nom comporte le mot poivre (sans parler du docteur), ce qui nécessite un certain aplomb. Pourtant, une publicité pour 7 UP®, qui a autant à gagner que Dr Pepper d'un message direct et bien ficelé, utilise une approche et une expression beaucoup moins conventionnelles : au lieu d'une photographie ou d'une peinture réaliste, l'agence utilise, astucieusement, une illustration conceptuelle où un homme regarde un match de football (à travers le prisme de ses jumelles), tandis que la bouteille est à peine suggérée (alors que, par convention, dans ce genre de publicité, on montrait le produit). Cela donne au spectateur un message supplémentaire à méditer, et c'était ça l'astuce. Peu à peu, les annonces de produits de consommation sont injectées de pointes d'originalité.

Cependant, la publicité des années 60 hérite de survivances des années 50 et qui marchent si bien, à l'époque d'Eisenhower,

qu'on aurait pu les garder jusqu'à l'émergence des jeux vidéo. Ainsi, la campagne pour Budweiser®, « Là où il y a de la vie, il y a de la Bud », se prolonge pendant presque une génération, et sans grands changements. Les images minutieusement mises en scène, de pépées sensuelles ou de play-boys gominés, attablés devant de grands verres pleins du breuvage mousseux, sont tellement ancrées dans l'imagerie populaire, que le magazine MAD, tristement célèbre pour ses pastiches publicitaires, en compose une parodie montrant un ivrogne mélancolique, et intitulée : « Pas très fier, mais très bière. » Malgré cette critique, s'assurer un slogan, un indicatif sonore ou un logo profondément inscrit dans la langue américaine, garantit une publicité gratuite.

Les années 60 donnent naissance à leurs propres classiques construits sur des titres et des slogans astucieux, destinés à s'infiltrer dans le subconscient des masses. Beaucoup restent inoffensifs, d'autres insipides. Parmi ces derniers, les plus mémorables sont souvent ceux consacrés aux cigarettes, comme celui-ci, pour les cigarettes à bout filtre Lucky Strike : « Montrez-moi une cigarette filtre qui mérite son titre

et je suis prêt(e) à avaler mon chapeau ! »
Si la blague semble laborieuse, elle devient
inoubliable quand elle est accouplée à la
photo d'un ravissant mannequin, coiffé d'un
chapeau auquel manque un grand morceau,
emporté par une morsure. Dans cette campagne, qui dure longtemps, une autre publicité montre une Viêtnamienne qui sourit
timidement sous son couvre-chef tradition-
nel en paille, et ce sera l'un des rares petits
coups de chapeau, si l'on peut dire, à l'engagement politique américain en Asie du
Sud-Est (vue, entre autres, comme terrain
idéal pour écouler la surproduction de
cigarettes). Autre publicité marquante de
l'époque, et constante thématique de
l'expression américaine, la campagne «
Soyez amis, buvez Pepsi ». Dans la plupart
de ces annonces, on voit des images photo
réalistes de jeunes bourgeois « sociables »
qui « préfèrent Pepsi », quand ils batifolent
sur les pistes de ski et dans les penthouses
de l'Amérique. Non seulement cette publicité encourage son public cible à vivre dans le
plaisir, mais le slogan va devenir le mantra
de toute une génération.

Certaines annonces sont considérées
comme des classiques parce que, d'une

manière ou d'une autre, elles ont favorisé
un style de vie devenu partie intégrante de
l'esprit du temps. La publicité pour Clairol,
par exemple, impose à chaque femme la
nécessité sociale de changer sa couleur de
cheveux, et le slogan « Le fait-elle ou pas ? Il
n'y a que son coiffeur qui le sait ! » souligne
à quel point c'est facile et efficace. D'autres,
pourtant, deviennent des classiques parce
qu'elles changent réellement la façon dont
le public voit son environnement. Le slogan
de Braniff, la compagnie aérienne interna-
tionale, « La fin ordonnée de l'avion
ordinaire », offre à un vieux produit une
nouvelle aura. En fait, c'est le produit qui
devient un véritable panneau publicitaire.
Pour rendre un petit avion portugais plus
attrayant à un large segment de la clientèle
américaine, on change la couleur des avions
eux-mêmes, qui passent de l'habituel gris
métallique à des couleurs primaires et
pastel. Le changement n'a rien à voir
avec la qualité du service, mais il signale
néanmoins une révolution perçue au ciel
comme sur terre : une compagnie aérienne
n'est pas uniquement un transporteur
impersonnel et utilitaire mais un cadre de
vie excitant (et coloré).

La publicité ne sera jamais neutre. Elle
doit toujours démontrer qu'une chose est
meilleure qu'une autre, et que celle-ci est
également la meilleure. Pendant les années
60, la définition de la vente offensive passe
du déferlement de mots et d'images re-
battus sur la tête du consommateur à une
créativité malicieuse, dont le but avoué
consiste à mieux faire entendre la publicité.
Et cela a fonctionné. Mais indépendamment
de la méthode, les publicités présentées
dans cet ouvrage – véritables vecteurs de
l'économie capitaliste – sont régies par
une priorité élémentaire : parvenir à une
identification si évidente que le public va
réclamer, désirer et exiger tout ce qu'on
veut lui vendre. C'est cela, en un mot, la
Grande Idée.

Steven Heller est l'auteur et l'éditeur de plus
de 80 livres sur la conception graphique et
la culture populaire, parmi lesquels : *Design
Literacy : Understanding Graphic Design*
(L'alphabétisation du design : comprendre
le design graphique), *The Graphic Design
Reader* (Manuel de design graphique), *Graphic Style : From Victorian to Digital* (Le style
graphique : du victorien au numérique), et
*Counter Culture : The Allure of Mini-Manne-
quins* (Contre-culture : L'attrait des mini-
mannequins).

a publicidad en los años sesenta:

¿ué es la Gran Idea?

or Steven Heller

Si un historiador utilizara como única ente de referencia los anuncios incluidos i este libro para examinar y analizar los rbulentos años sesenta, obtendría una nagen de la cultura norteamericana poco el a la realidad social y política de la época.)ónde están los negros, los latinos y los iáticos? Contemplados desde este punto e vista estratégico, en los años sesenta no istieron las manifestaciones a favor de los erechos civiles, ni la guerra del Vietnam, ni amor libre, las drogas y el rock and roll, o, menos, no existieron de forma significati- . Los anuncios aquí expuestos, exhuma- os de las criptas de las agencias de adison Avenue –la llamada «avenida e la publicidad»– y recogidos tal y como areçían en las revistas de amplia difusión e entonces, conforman una publicidad éptica, homogeneizada y cauterizada, lo ial no implica que estuviera privada de stilo, buen gusto o humor, ni que no flejara el espíritu de la época con cierta osis de cinismo.

Al fin y al cabo, la publicidad no es más ue una verdad artificial. Si bien, evidente- ente, siempre parte de una idea cierta: el aquillaje oculta las imperfecciones del ros-

tro, la gaseosa es dulce, el mal aliento es desagradable, el dolor de cabeza es molesto y las gafas de sol protegen los ojos. En la década de los sesenta, los anuncios de me- dicamentos y ungüentos milagrosos a base de aceite de serpiente tan populares a prin- cipios de siglo habían quedado totalmente erradicados. Sin embargo, la publicidad, en particular en aquella época, tenía por fin superar en ventas y reputación a la compe- tencia por todos los medios tolerables se- gún las llamadas doctrinas de la «publici- dad veraz», un concepto afín a permitir la presencia de una cantidad aceptable de pelo de rata en productos alimenticios. Las men- tiras y exageraciones abundaban, pero a nadie parecía importarle, ya que las imáge- nes, los eslóganes y las ideas rayaban la del- gada línea que separa la realidad de lo irri- sorio. Es más, a principios de los años sesenta, en plena posguerra, los norteame- ricanos estaban predispuestos a creer cie- gamente en todo lo que aparecía en los me- dios de comunicación de masas y aceptaban los anuncios sin ningún tipo de cuestiona- miento o duda. Por ello, muchos anuncios publicados en revistas y emitidos por la tele- visión se percibían más como una suerte de entretenimiento o pasatiempo que como meras armas para aumentar las ventas.

Durante la década de los años sesenta, la publicidad abandonó su predilección por los textos extensos y ampulosos para susti- tuirlos por combinaciones de imágenes y eslóganes con gancho, aplicando un méto- do conocido como la «Gran Idea». El térmi- no no sólo connota un punto de inflexión radical en relación con el pasado, sino que, además, define un género creativo genuina- mente norteamericano. Los pioneros de la llamada «Revolución Creativa», de la que emergió la Gran Idea, intuyeron que, para captar la atención del público y lograr calar en el imaginario popular, sus mensajes tení- an que ser divertidos, lo cual llevó a las agencias de publicidad de Madison Avenue a hacerse con algunas armas propagandísti- cas, como la contratación de grandes talen- tos, entre otras.

La imagen del arma sirve perfectamente como metáfora porque, al fin y al cabo, una campaña publicitaria no es distinta de una maniobra en un campo de batalla. Cuanto más eficaz sea la artillería, mejor sea la estrategia y mayor sea el contingente, más serán los cerebros y los corazones conquis- tados. El bombardeo incesante de eslóga- nes e imágenes redujo claramente la resis- tencia y afianzó la identificación de las marcas comerciales. Si el producto vendido cumplía lo anunciado, tanto mejor; aunque, cuando la batalla no tenía contrincante, ni siquiera era necesario que lo hiciera. Basta, si no, con echar una ojeada a los anuncios de algunas de las marcas preponderantes de los años sesenta, entre ellas: Maiden- form®, Anacin®, General Electric y Clairol. Aunque los productos eran verdaderamente eficaces, el aura y los falsos mitos que los envolvían les concedían un estatus y un atractivo para las ventas que les reportaban una amplia cuota de mercado, hasta que otro fabricante los desafiaba con un canto de sirena aún más embaucador. El destino de los productos existentes cambiaba de rumbo cuando una nueva marca lanzaba una campaña publicitaria más perspicaz e implacable, haciendo gala de lo que en el argot de Madison Avenue se conoce como «creatividad» espectacular.

Un ejemplo claro es la campaña de los años sesenta de Volkswagen, obra de Doyle Dane Bernbach, quien fue capaz de tomar un pequeño automóvil «para el pueblo» creado a finales de los años treinta bajo el auspicio de Adolf Hitler y convertirlo instantáneamente en el coche más vendido entre una población amante de los automóviles de grandes dimensiones, con tan sólo anunciar que las carencias aparentes del vehículo eran en realidad sus verdaderas ventajas. Una muestra excelente de ingenio estratégico y publicidad brillante. Otro ejemplo es el anuncio del televisor portátil Sony, un aparato diminuto fabricado en Japón (otro adversario en la época de preguerra), cuna de los transistores baratos, que, gracias a una imagen y un eslogan ocurrentes, propulsó a la marca a competir directamente con las pantallas de gran formato estadounidenses.

A lo largo de los años sesenta, la Gran Idea dotó la publicidad de una inteligencia, humor y elegancia jamás vistos en el pasado. Los wunderkinder (chicos maravillosos) de Madison Avenue sentaron nuevas bases.

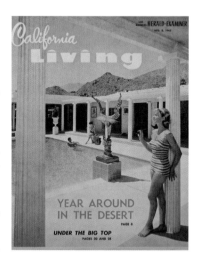

Directores artísticos como George Lois, Gene Federico, Bill Taubin, Helmut Krone, Bob Gage y otros muchos supieron apreciar el poder inherente a la tipografía y las imágenes de calidad, y lo utilizaron para dotar sus anuncios de un toque de elegancia y clase que les valió el respeto del público. No obstante, sus singulares anuncios no eran sino auténticas perlas en medio de un gran magma de burdas piedras. La década de los sesenta fue un período de transición en el que la Revolución Creativa se enfrentó a un statu quo mediocre, aunque no por ello poco profesional. Producir un anuncio típico, por ejemplo el de salchichas Premium de la marca Swift –en el que una madre modélica y sus dos hijos, universitarios impolutos, se disputaban amistosamente el manjar en una composición propia de una ilustración de Norman Rockwell–, requería una inversión de capital y energía considerable. Y, sin embargo, aparentemente sus creadores carecían de la visión y la intuición necesarias para apreciar que incluso un anuncio prototípico de un producto tan cotidiano como son las salchichas permitía utilizar el ingenio para trascender el cliché. Del mismo modo, pese a su simplicidad insul-

tante, el anuncio de refrescos Dr. Pepper de principios de los años sesenta supuso un arduo trabajo para la agencia de publicidad que lo creó. Mostrando a una joven sedienta que soñaba con beberse otro Pepper, la marca intentaba arañar una parte del mercado a Coke® y Pepsi®. El mero hecho de conseguir que la boca, los ojos y el pelo de la modelo resultaran lo suficientemente atractivos como para incitar a alguien a tomarse un refresco llamado Dr. Pepper (literalmente Doctor Pimienta) implicaba desplegar una dosis considerable de autoestima desmedida. En cambio, el anuncio de 7 UP®, que se enfrentaba a los mismos anuncios de calidad demostrada que Dr. Pepper, recurrió a un enfoque expresivo mucho menos convencional: en lugar de utilizar una fotografía o una ilustración realista, rompió esquemas al usar una ilustración conceptual de un hombre viendo un partido de fútbol (reflejado en los cristales de sus prismáticos) en la que la botella del refresco apenas aparecía esbozada (en una época en la que la convención era mostrar el producto), lo cual transmitía al espectador un mensaje que le invitaba a la reflexión. Poco a poco, los anuncios para el gran público empezaron a exhibir mayores dosis de originalidad.

Con todo, la publicidad de los años sesenta heredó algunos vestigios de los años cincuenta que habían funcionado tan bien durante la era de Eisenhower que no había necesidad de cambiarlos en la era de Camelot. La campaña de Budweiser®, «Donde hay vida, hay Bud» se perpetuó con leves modificaciones, al menos, una generación más. Las ilustraciones hiperrealistas de mujeres sensuales y seductores playboys contemplando con ojos ávidos cómo les servían tubos de cerveza espumosa habían arraigado de tal modo en la cultura estadounidense que la revista MAD, de infausta fama por sus parodias de anuncios, publicó una ilustración en la que aparecía un borracho en estado lamentable bajo el lema «Budweiser no da la felicidad, pero contribuye». Pese a sus connotaciones críticas, e

cho de mostrar un eslogan, una música o
□ logotipo que formara parte indeleble del
□aginario estadounidense constituía una
□pecie de publicidad gratuita.

Pero los años sesenta también incuba-
□n sus propios clásicos, arraigados en los
□ulares elaborados y las coletillas concebi-
□s para conquistar el subconsciente del
□blico general. Muchas de estas frases
□an inocuas; otras, sencillamente insípidas.
□tre las últimas, las más memorables eran
□s eslóganes de cigarrillos, entre ellos el de
□cky Strike, que rezaba «Prometo que el
□a que encuentre un rubio de verdad, me
□meré el sombrero». Pese a la rigidez apa-
□nte de la redacción, el lema calaba hondo
□aparecer estampado sobre la fotografía de
□a atractiva modelo tocada con un som-
□ero mordido. En uno de los anuncios de
□a extensa campaña, una vietnamita son-
□a tímidamente bajo un sombrero de paja
□ico de su región, en lo que tal vez supo-
□a una insinuación de la implicación geo-
□lítica de Estados Unidos en el Sudeste
□iático (como vertedero de cigarrillos,
□tre otras cosas). Otro anuncio monumen-
□ de la época y un tema recurrente en la
□ltura norteamericana fue la campaña

«Ten clase, bebe Pepsi». Gran parte de los
anuncios incluían ilustraciones hiperrealistas de jóvenes de clase media bebiendo una
Pepsi en los refugios de las pistas de esquí
o en lujosos áticos. Además de invitar al
público al que iba destinado a vivir la vida
con estilo, el eslogan se convirtió en un
mantra para toda una generación.

Algunos anuncios se consideran clásicos porque, de algún modo, impulsaron un
estilo de vida que se convirtió en parte integral del espíritu de la época. Los anuncios
de Clairol, sin ir más lejos, lograron conver-
tir los tintes de pelo en un imperativo social
para toda mujer, gracias al eslogan «¿Se
tiñe o no se tiñe? Sólo su peluquera lo
sabe», que subrayaba lo fácil y eficaz que
resultaba teñirse el pelo. En cambio, otros
anuncios se han convertido en clásicos porque cambiaron realmente la percepción del
entorno por parte del público. Con el lema
«Asista al final del avión convencional», las
líneas aéreas Braniff International presenta-
ron un producto antiguo envuelto en una
nueva aura. En realidad, el producto en sí
servía de valla publicitaria. Con el fin de
atraer a un amplio segmento de los viajeros
norteamericanos, esta pequeña compañía
aérea portuguesa cambió el habitual color
metálico de sus aviones por varios tonos
primarios y pastel. Y aunque dicho cambio
poco tenía que ver con la provisión de un
servicio mejor, marcó una revolución tanto
en el cielo como en la tierra, pues logró
transmitir la idea de que una compañía de
líneas aéreas no era sólo un transporte utili-
tario e impersonal, sino toda una experien-
cia (cromática).

La publicidad nunca será neutra, ya
que su fin es demostrar que un producto
es mejor que otro, o aún más: que el producto anunciado es el mejor. Durante los
años sesenta se redefinió el concepto de
ventas agresivas: se pasó de bombardear al
consumidor con comentarios e imágenes
populares a recurrir a juegos creativos pre-
sumiblemente destinados a que el público
se sintiera más incentivado por los anuncios. Y funcionó. Pero, independientemente

del método que emplean, los anuncios ilus-
trados en este volumen –la verdadera co-
lumna vertebral de una economía capitalista
dirigida por el mercado– respondían a una
única meta: construir una imagen comercial
incomparable y perfectamente identificable
por el público que suscitara el clamor, el
deseo y la demanda, al margen de cuál fuera
el producto vendido. Y, en pocas palabras,
ésa es la Gran Idea.

Steven Heller es autor y editor de más de
ochenta libros sobre diseño gráfico y cultura
popular, entre los que se cuentan: *Design
Literacy: Understanding Graphic Design*, *The
Graphic Design Reader*, *Graphic Style: From
Victorian to Digital* y *Counter Culture: The
Allure of Mini-Mannequins*.

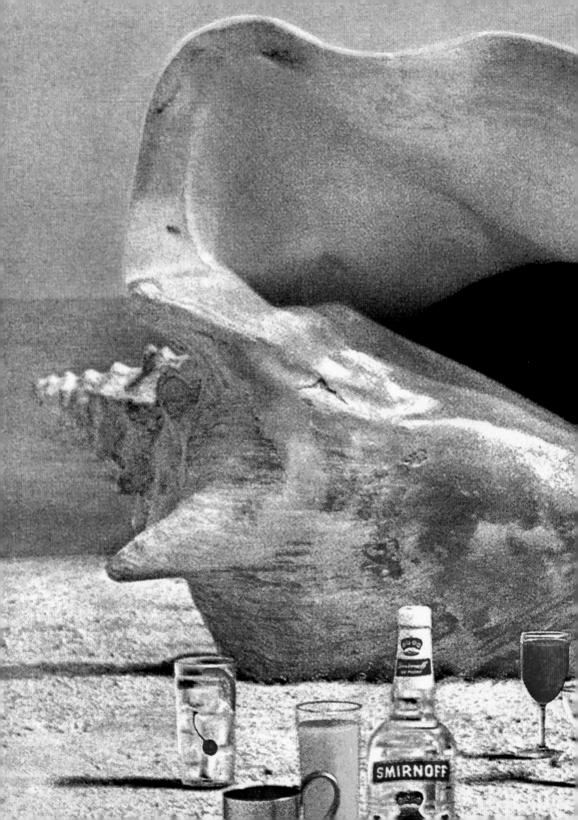

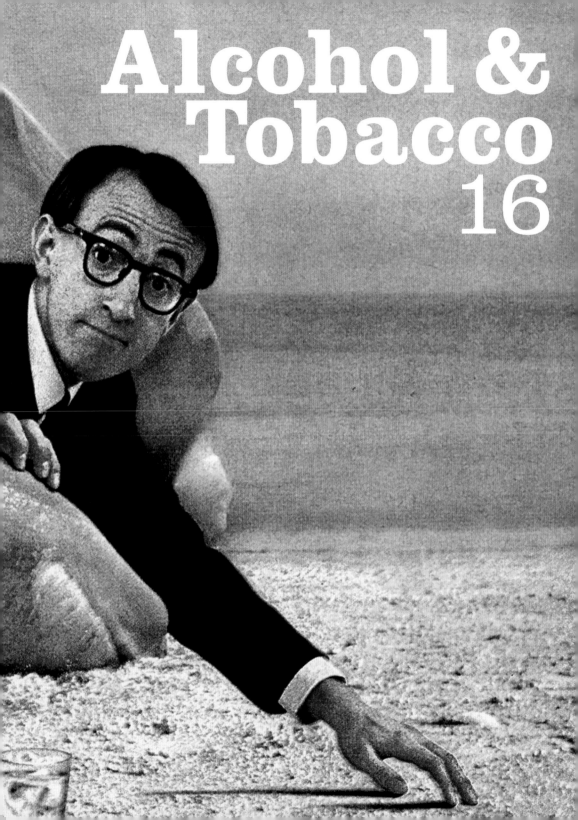

Alcohol & Tobacco

16

Burgie II

A warm day . . . a cool breeze . . . plenty of easygoing Burgie. And in light, refreshing Burgermeister Beer you'll find the extra touch of quality that means the difference between the very good and the very best. A difference you can describe in just four words—

So much more refreshing!

this calls for

Budweiser

*the neighbors...*out in the kitchen, swapping ideas with good friends. This is fun ...and <u>this</u> calls for Budweiser.

Where there's life...there's Bud.

HAVEN'T TRIED SMIRNOFF? WHERE IN THE WORLD HAVE YOU BEEN?

You've really been out of touch if you haven't explored Smirnoff with orange juice, with tomato juice, with 7-Up® (in the new Smirnoff Mule). Or discovered that Smirnoff makes the dryest Martinis, the smoothest drink on-the-rocks. Only Smirnoff, filtered through 14,000 pounds of activated charcoal, makes so many drinks so well. Why wait? Let the next Smirnoff launching be *yours!*

Always ask for *Smirnoff* VODKA *It leaves you breathless*®

Get acquainted offer: Try the delicious drinks you've been missing with this new half quart sampler bottle. Now available in most states.

80 AND 100 PROOF. DISTILLED FROM GRAIN. STE. PIERRE SMIRNOFF FLS. (DIVISION OF HEUBLEIN), HARTFORD, CONN.

Smirnoff

Rudi Gernreich fashions the breathless scene. And women start turning up in colors beautiful enough to drink. Bloody Mary Red. Blizzard Lime. Screwdriver Orange. Mule Copper. And Martini Silver. Pick your favorite Smirnoff drink. Then pick a woman to match.

Smirnoff Vodka leaves you breathless.

Ron Rico. Wasn't he the international jewel thief who ravaged the Riviera right after the war?

Round the world rage, yes. Ruffian, never. Ronrico's a rum. The very light, very dry Puerto Rican rum. With the very smooth taste.

Steal out and pick up a bottle. You have nothing to lose but your heart.

For a 30" x 40" color poster of this ad send $1 to Personality Posters, Dept. L-9, 74 Fifth Ave., NYC 10011. Void where prohibited.

Ronrico. A rum to remember.

©1968 GENERAL WINE AND SPIRITS COMPANY, NYC. 80 PROOF

Ronrico, 1968

▶ *Cinzano, 1966*   ▶ ▶ *Holland House Cocktail Mixes, 1964*

Monroe, don't be angry because I told the girls we hired an expert bartender for our party. You are going to make the drinks with Holland House Cocktail Mixes. And doesn't that make you an expert?

With Holland House Cocktail Mixes and your own good liquor, what a drink maker you'll be! What a host! What a hero to your guests! When they taste your superb Whiskey Sours, Gimlets, Manhattans, Old Fashioneds, Daiquiris, Tom Collins, Bloody Marys, Martinis and Side Cars, they'll think you've hired a professional bartender.

And you'll think our mixes are some kind of magic potions.

We start with only the finest ingredients. Natural, fresh-squeezed citrus juices shipped directly from sunny groves in California and Trinidad.

Concentrated juices wouldn't cost as much but your drinks wouldn't taste as fresh.

We also bring exotic herbs, roots and spices from all over the world. Sure it costs more to import them, but you can taste the extra care and expense in every cocktail. All 9 mixes are at food stores everywhere, liquor stores in some states. An 89¢ bottle* makes dozens of sensational drinks. Bloody Mary is 59¢ a quart.*

Whiskey Sour, Manhattan, Daiquiri, Collins, Gimlet, Old Fashioned, Martini, Side Car, Bloody Mary.

You make the best drinks you ever tasted with

HOLLAND HOUSE COCKTAIL MIXES
Original and largest selling in the world.

CINZANO
imported, of course
IMPORTED FROM FRANCE
EXTRA DRY
CINZANO
FRENCH
EXTRA DRY VERMOUTH
cdc
PARIS FRANCE
IMPORTED FROM ITALY
MELLOW
CINZANO
ITALIAN VERMOUTH
TORINO (Italy)
NATIONAL DISTILLERS PRODUCTS C°
NEW YORK N.Y.
mix with Cinzano and you mix with the best

Private Showing—and V.O. enhances the occasion with its flawless flavor and genuine talent for pleasing particular people.

KNOWN BY THE COMPANY IT KEEPS SEAGRAM'S

VO

IMPORTED
CANADIAN WHISKY

How to make a perfect Daiquiri in one minute flat

by Jerry and Anne Chase (who learned how at La Concha in Puerto Rico)

WE used to think only bartenders and beach-combers could make a perfect daiquiri. Then one afternoon a friendly bartender at the new La Concha Hotel taught us how to mix a delicious daiquiri in just one minute. Here's the way it's done:

Squeeze half a lime. (Time: twenty seconds for the most inept.) Add a half teaspoon of sugar. (Can that take more than five seconds?) Pour in a jigger of dry, white rum from Puerto Rico. (Another twenty seconds, allowing plenty of time to check the label for the magic words "Puerto Rican Rum.")

Shake well with ice and pour. (Fifteen seconds if you are patient.) And there you have it —on the rocks or off. The perfect daiquiri in one minute.

Shopping Guide: When you buy rum, look for the words "Puerto Rican Rum" on the label. your guide to perfect daiquiris. For a free booklet of exciting rum recipes, write Rums of Puerto Rico, Dept. G-8, 666 Fifth Ave., N. Y. 19, N. Y.

"But, Daddy, if I don't drink they'll think I'm nowhere."

Now, Dad, what do you say to that?

You could say, and with conviction, that what they think really won't matter. Not if she's sure the way you've taught her is right.

But make no mistake. She's under a lot of pressure from others her own age. Social pressure to be popular—to be one of the crowd. It would be unrealistic to think otherwise.

To stand up to that kind of pressure takes character. And character isn't something a girl is born with. It's something she acquires. Mostly from you, her parents.

If you've taught her well—if you've set a good example, she'll understand that drinking is a pleasure reserved for adults.

She can wait. She has time.

And when that time comes, if she chooses to drink, she'll appreciate drinking for what it is. Something to be enjoyed sensibly. Moderately. Maturely. The way we've always intended the products we sell be enjoyed.

A Father's Day message from...**Seagram / distillers since 1857**

For reprints, please write: Advertising Dept., Seagram Distillers Co., 375 Park Ave., N.Y., N.Y. 10022

Seagram's, 1967

▶ *Fleischmann's, 1962*

NOW:

Everything to make it happen comes inside the bottle. Uncap the new free spirit in liquor. 17 uninhibited drinks from Heublein—all very strong on flavor. The finest liquor and bar mixings in the whole drinking world come right in the bottle. Nothing to squeeze, measure, mix or add. Just pour over ice.

Heublein®
ADVENTUROUS COCKTAILS

Mai-Tai, Margarita, Black Russian, Daiquiri, Gimlet, Stinger, Side Car, Old Fashioned, Manhattan. Four Sours: Whiskey, Vodka, Tequila and Apricot. Four Martinis: Two Gin and Two Vodka. 50-75 Proof. Heublein, Inc., Hartford Conn.

"Us Tareyton smokers would rather fight than switch!"

Join the Unswitchables. Get the filter that made
Activated Charcoal famous—and the taste that makes
Tareyton smokers so aggressively loyal.

Fine
granules of
Activated Charcoal
in pure
cellulose

The white filter gives you clean taste

The charcoal filter gives you smooth taste

Together they give you the great taste of

DUAL FILTER TAREYTON

America's largest-selling Activated Charcoal filter cigarette

Product of *The American Tobacco Company*—*Tobacco is our middle name* © A. T. Co.

**NOW
IN NEW
POP-OPEN
PACK**

Tareyton
The American Tobacco Company
DUAL FILTER

Put out the bottle that shows you know SCOTCH!
Enjoy the extra smoothness that has always given
"Black & White" a light, bright character all its own.

"BLACK & WHITE" *Scotch*
THE SCOTCH WITH CHARACTER

DISTILLED AND BOTTLED IN SCOTLAND · BLENDED SCOTCH WHISKY · 86.8 PROOF · THE FLEISCHMANN DISTILLING CORPORATION, NEW YORK CITY · SOLE DISTRIBUTORS

Black & White, 1961

▶ *Walker's, 1962*

A city half-lost

in twilight, between the sea and the sky.
In a gentle time, a dreaming time. A time
most amiably matched by the mellow
elegance of Walker's DeLuxe – eight years old
and the finest bourbon an evening ever found.

STRAIGHT BOURBON WHISKEY · 86.8 PROOF · HIRAM WALKER & SONS INC., PEORIA, ILL.

Old Taylor 86, 1963

Old Taylor 86, 1963

Old Taylor 86, 1964

Old Taylor 86, 1964   ▶ Jim Beam, 1966

The gift is distinctive.
The season is merry.
The man is Sean Connery.
The Bourbon is JIM BEAM.

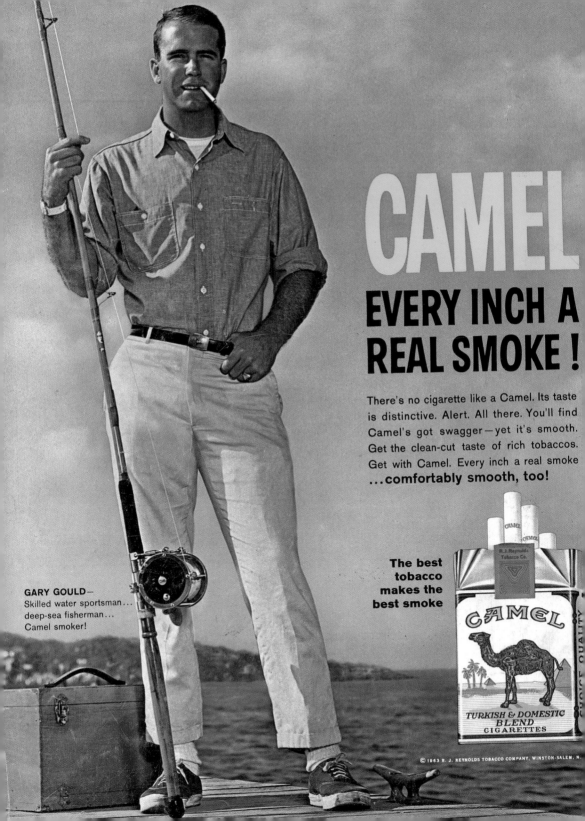

Marlboro Country. There's not another place like it. You get a bigger helping of flavor here. The tobacco in Marlboro's famous Richmond Recipe tastes richer... smoother, too, through the exclusive Selectrate® Filter. You get a lot to like: **a man's world of flavor in a filter cigarette.**

Auto–
mobiles
38

Some people own cars.

Some cars own people.

OLD WAY: two pieces, body and frame, bolted together. This method is going out of date.   NEW WAY: one welded piece. The Plymouth Unibody is tight, roomy, quiet and durable.

We built the Solid '60 Plymouth for those who want to be boss.

Any car costs money to run. But it needn't "own" you.

You should spend very little to keep up the new Solid Plymouth. Chrysler Corporation engineers designed it around new Dura-Quiet Unibody construction—a better way of building that uses about 5400 vise-tight welds to unite body and undersills. They developed new processes to lick rust and corrosion. They improved Plymouth's lively standard V-8 that topped its low-price class in the Mobilgas Economy Run the past three years in a row.

Try this money-saving Plymouth soon.

A Chrysler-engineered product, built a new solid way to give you solid satisfaction.

SOLID PLYMOUTH 1960

See "THE STEVE ALLEN PLYMOUTH SHOW," *Monday nights,* NBC-TV. *Solid!*

HE
wanted a Fiat Spider

SHE
wanted a Fiat "600"

The FIAT 1200 SPIDER is all the car a man could want. A tiger on the road. Stunning Italian styling by Pinin Farina. Careful Italian craftsmanship in every detail. A humming 1221 cc. engine that delivers plenty of zip and about 27 miles a gallon. Roll-up windows, plenty of legroom, tuck-away soft top and optional hard top too, if you want it. Best of all, a price tag that lets you drive it instead of dream about it — only $2595*. (And it's the only car also available with the winging new version of a famous 1.5 liter racing engine! WHOOSH!)

THEY
got them
both

(...and saved a garageful of money!)

The FIAT 600 is everyone's ideal car, perfect for scooting to the supermarket, dropping the kids off at school, or taking the whole family to grandma's for the weekend. It parks in spaces that don't look big enough for a bike. Delivers about 40 miles a gallon. Includes almost $300† worth of accessories at no extra charge. And costs only $1398* — about $200 less than the leading French and German imports.

SPIDER or 600, a FIAT will keep your family happy. Your budget, too. Try either one tomorrow. Better yet, try both.

†Accessories included at no extra charge: heater, defroster, whitewalls, windshield washers, electric wipers, turn signals, undercoating, leatherette interiors, fold-down rear seats.
*Suggested prices, port of entry, New York. Sales and service throughout U.S. and Canada. 18 Fiat models to choose from. Suggested prices start as low as $1098 p.o.e. New York; slightly higher on West Coast.

For overseas delivery or rental, see your nearest Fiat Dealer, travel agent, or write to the Fiat Motor Company, Inc., 500 Fifth Ave., New York 36, N.Y.
A product of Turin, cradle of ITALIAN unity. Visit Turin and the Italian Centennial Exhibition, May through October, 1961.

The liveliest, most care-free cars of the year are here!

See the greatest auto show ever assembled under one dealer's banner—at your Ford Dealer's! For '63 there are four complete lines of fine cars from Ford! 44 different models, including the first Falcon convertible! The brand-new Ford Fairlane wagons and hardtops! The new Super Torque Ford Galaxie! The most luxurious Thunderbird ever! Turn the page and start the fun.

R EXTRA QUIET AND COMFORT IN YOUR NEW CAR . . . MAKE THE

QUIET TEST

EST NEW CARS GIVE YOU EXTRA PROTECTION AGAINST SOUNDS AND MOTOR VIBRATIONS WITH SPECIAL FIBERGLAS INSULATION.

you decide on that new car . . . feel the inside of the roof. If it's soft and
t, you're feeling sound-insulation. Owens-Corning Fiberglas automotive
ion is basically the same insulation used in high altitude jet airliners to
e protection against noise and temperature. Many of the best 1960 cars use
as* Insulation under the roof . . . under the hood . . . behind the motor.
nber . . . Fiberglas Insulation absorbs the noise and assures extra driving
rt. Be sure to make the "Quiet Test" at your local automobile dealer.
-Corning Fiberglas Corporation, Dept. 10D-11, Toledo 1, Ohio.

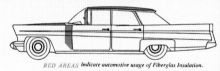

RED AREAS indicate automotive usage of Fiberglas Insulation.

OWENS-CORNING
FIBERGLAS

*T. M. (Reg. U. S. Pat. Off.) O-C. F. Corp.

Oldsmobile, 1960

Fiberglas, 1960 ◀ Oldsmobile, 1960

▶ *Cadillac, 1960* ▶▶ *Chrysler, 1960* ▶▶▶ *Plymouth, 1961*

Cadillac

THE CADILLAC "V" AND CREST interpreted in Rubies and Diamonds BY HARRY WINSTON, IN

Where Craftsmanship is a Creed!

There are, to be sure, many ways to learn the story of Cadillac craftsmanship. But the best of these—and certainly the most enjoyable —is simply to inspect and drive a 1960 Cadillac. Every exquisite detail of its interior, for instance, reveals a skill and care in execution that is unique in motordom. Every graceful, tight-fitting body line evidences the rare devotion lavished on its final assembly. And every silent, solid mile on the highway speaks eloquently of Cadillac's great overall soundness of construction. We suggest you visit your dealer soon—and see for yourself how fine a motor car can be when craftsmanship is the irrevocable creed of its maker.

CADILLAC MOTOR CAR DIVISION • GENERAL MOTORS CORPORATION

1960 CHRYSLER - THE CAR OF YOUR LIFE FO

Chrysler Saratoga 4-Door Hardtop in sizzling Toreador Red. Power steering and brakes, automatic transmission standard equipment.

Marion & John:
A wonderful trip! the new Chrysler's so smooth, decided to drive straight through. Roger delighted til I made him give up the wheel. Just had to drive it! Love those pushbuttons. Still wish you'd both come along. Loads of room—for you and gear. Use this card for raincheck.
Love
Jane and Roger

P.S. Count on us next Sunday at 7 (thanks to the Chrysler.)

Mr. & Mrs. John Gahagan
16 Quail Hollow Dr.
Farmington
Mich.

IE TIME OF YOUR LIFE!

Announcing the most beautiful turn of the

61 PLYMOU

tury! **Plymouth for '61!**

Never before a Plymouth so dramatically new and different! See and feel the head start it gives you into 1961, with its startling new looks, its eagerness, its sureness, its tight snug quality. Beneath the all-new lines is the Solid Plymouth Unibody—one-piece, welded, tough and quiet. So get with the newest! Get with '61 Plymouth—at your dealer's now!

H...SOLID BEAUTY

erica's No. 1 low-price economy car...a Chrysler-engineered product

17th century brocade from Detroit Institute of Arts

Jeweled "V" and Crest created by Black, Starr and C

In beauty and in performance, the 1961 Cadillac represents a new standard by which the world's motor cars will be judged.

CADILLAC MOTOR CAR DIVISION, GENERAL MOTORS CORPO

Cadillac

8th Century embroidery from The Brooklyn Museum   The Fleetwood 60 Special   Jeweled "V" and Crest created by Cartier

The highest praise that can be accorded any product in any field is to declare it the Cadillac of its kind.

Skyrocket!

A fiery new class of cars is here . . . Oldsmobile for '61! Sparked by the spirit of an exciting new *SKYROCKET* Engine—blazing a bright new trail in automotive performance!

Oldsmobile . . . with a completely new and smoother-than-ever Hydra-Matic Drive* featuring Accel-A-Rotor action for quick, silken getaway!

Oldsmobile . . . with crisp, sleek style that reflects its flashing performance . . . and the roomiest, most glamorous, easiest-to-get-into interiors you ever saw!

All this is exclusively yours in the spirited new Olds for 1961

. . . featuring Fashion-Line design and *SKYROCKET* performance!

Join the style leaders in a new '61 Olds . . . at your dealer's now!

OLDSMOBILE DIVISION OF GENERAL MOTORS CORPORATION   *Optional at extra cost.*

OLDSMOBILE
Super 88

More spirited than ever for '61!

What makes a Pontiac so eager to go?

This Catalina has more horsepower per pound than any other automatic transmission car made in America. (As much as one horse per 10.65 pounds.) That's an ideal balance between weight and power. Gives you hustle when you need it. Improves gas mileage, too. Eager to go? Go see your fine Pontiac dealer.

LIKE MAGIC...

YOU'LL FEEL BETTER, LOOK NEATER, STAY CLEAN
WITH GENERAL MOTORS CAR AIR CONDITION[

Go the healthful way—with Harrison Air Conditioning you breathe air that's literally wa
... cool, invigorating air! This refreshing atmosphere helps take the tension out of ever
traffic ... the stress and strain out of all-day trips. What's more, you'll enjoy refre
new relief from pollen and other air-borne irritants. *Go the neat way*—Harrison Air
ditioning eliminates excess humidity ... clothes hold a sharp press, collars never wilt
keeps that combed-and-brushed freshness. *Go the clean way*—your car's interior can
spick-and-span as your living room. With Harrison Air Conditioning, you lock out
grime and insects ... you knock out the road and wind noise that disturbs radio liste
and conversation. So for a *healthier*, *cleaner*, *neater* way to go for you and your family
ask your GM Dealer for Harrison Air Conditioning in your new Cadillac, Buick,
mobile, Pontiac or Chevrolet.

*COMPRESSOR BY FRIGI[

cool air by the carload

GM HARRISON
AUTOMOTIVE AIR CONDITIONING

ASK YOUR GENERAL MOTORS DEALER FOR A
DEMONSTRATION

HARRISON RADIATOR DIVISION, GENERAL MOTORS CORPORATION, LOCKPORT, NEW YO

AUTOMOTIVE RADIATORS • OIL COOLERS • THERMOSTATS • AIR CONDITIONERS • HEATERS • DEFROSTE

Are they making the turnpikes shorter this year?

Take that next trip in a '61 Plymouth. This Solid Beauty will give you a feeling that roads have never been so smooth, horizons so easy to catch. Everything about this low-price car takes you there in new comfort. It's easy to get in, easy to sit in, easy to see out of. Its quiet one-piece welded Unibody is snug and tight. Its Torsion-Aire suspension (no extra cost) takes practically all the sway and dip out of driving. Plymouth is smoothing the kinks out of the miles. Let your Plymouth dealer show you how.

'61 PLYMOUTH...SOLID BEAUTY

There's nothing like

Springtime...in a Rocket!

Your world is brighter . . . your heart is lighter . . . when you get out and go in a '60 Olds!
There's more thrill to the smooth performance of the great Rocket Engine. More sure-footed stability
with Quadri-Balanced Ride . . . the *quietest* you've ever tried. And what style . . . what models . . . what colors!
Look 'em over now at your Quality Dealer's.   OLDSMOBILE DIVISION • GENERAL MOTORS CORPORATION

GO OLDS '60

Oldsmobile, 1960

Announcing!

1961 SUPER 88 →

by OLDSMOBILE

The Action Line...in Performance and Design!

A glamorous all-new version
of Oldsmobile's super-performer... *more spirited than ever!*

Again Oldsmobile takes the initiative . . . in high style and high performance! New "Action-Line" design radiates the look
of luxury, the feel of flight . . . brings you the full-size room you like! The exclusive combination of the exhilarating
new Skyrocket Engine and the all-new Hydra-Matic* with Accel-A-Rotor action writes a bright new chapter in
Oldsmobile-pioneered performance! Gorgeous new interiors sparkle with new fabrics. And the ride is "super" too . . .
cushioned in live rubber at more than 90 different points. Come try this spirited Super 88—and the Classic 98
or the dollar-saving Dynamic 88—all on gala display at your Oldsmobile Quality Dealer's now!   *optional at extra cost.
Oldsmobile Division of General Motors Corporation.

General Motors, 1961 ◄◄ Plymouth, 1961 ◄ Oldsmobile, 1961   ► Pontiac, 1961

Meet the *Scout*!
A whole new idea in low-cost transportation...

Here's America's new quick-change artist. In minutes you can make your INTERNATIONAL Scout whatever kind of vehicle you want. The cab top, doors and windows are readily removable; the windshield folds down. No other vehicle is so changeable <u>and</u> so storm-snug. Then there's the full-length Travel-Top. Now the Scout can become a multi-purpose delivery unit or convertible, a light-duty pickup or runabout.

It's a working partner, a pleasure companion. You can buy the new Scout with two-wheel-drive or four-wheel-drive,

depending on the roads you travel or the jobs you want done. Take your friends hunting in rough country, take the family on a picnic, haul loads. And the Scout is <u>compact</u>: less than 13 feet overall, 100-inch wheelbase, 68 inches wide, 67 inches high. New INTERNATIONAL Comanche 4-cyl. 90 hp. engine goes easy on gas, oil, and upkeep.

Let your imagination roam—isn't the Scout the only one that spans *all* your needs? Your INTERNATIONAL Scout Dealer or Branch is the place to go to find out everything you can do with the Scout.

This is the Scout, a neat, nimble pickup with 5-ft. long loadspace.

Same Scout with cab top off. Takes you only minutes to remove.

Same Scout stripped, with doors and windows off, windshield down.

Same Scout for delivery work with optional full-length Travel-Top.

International Harvester Company,

The XP-755 Chevrolet Corvette Shark: 102.1" wheelbase, 192.2" overall, 327-cubic-inch displacement, V-8 engine featuring Roots-type supercharger, 4 side-draft carburetors developing over 400 horsepower.

Shark by Chevrolet—ACtion sparked by AC

The same AC Spark Plugs that add power to this car of tomorrow are available for your car today! Engineers specify ACs for experimental cars like the Corvette Shark because of AC's self-cleaning Hot Tip. It heats faster to burn away fouling carbon deposits — delivers longer peak power — greater economy for every car! Don't experiment with your spark plugs, ask for ACtion . . . ask for AC.

AC SPARK PLUG ⟡ THE ELECTRONICS DIVISION OF GENERAL MOTORS

AC

FIRE-RING
SPARK PLUGS

Starfire ...sensation of the year!

by OLDS

Everyone's talking about the new Starfire . . . because there's nothing else like it! Oldsmobile's spectacular new full-size sports convertible is custom-crafted with contoured bucket seats and center control console. And it's powered for the adventurous . . . with ultra-high compression, multijet carburetion, high performance camshaft and high-torque rear axle! See what all the excitement's about . . . at your Olds Quality Dealer's!

OLDSMOBILE DIVISION • GENERAL MOTORS CORPORATION

Standard Equipment: Sports-type control console • Tachometer • Hydra-Matic with stick control • Power windows • Power steering • Power brakes • Power seat • Starfire Engine with 10.25-to-1 compression ratio • 440 lb.-ft. torque at 2800 r.p.m. • 330 H.P. at 4600 r.p.m. • Dual exhaust system • Fiberpacked mufflers • High-performance 3.42-to-1 rear axle ratio • Twin top-grain leather bucket seats • Color-matched luggage compartment • Embossed aluminum side moulding • White sidewall tires • Wheelbase, 123″• Over-all length, 212″.

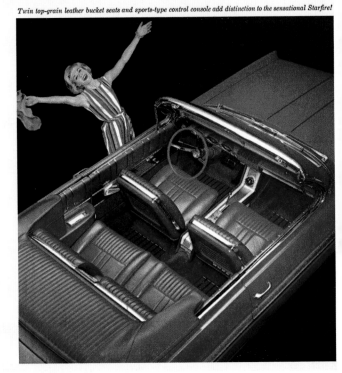

The new Mercedes-Benz 220 SE Coupe photographed at Helbrun Castle in Austria

Coupe d'Etat

For over half a century, it has been the pleasure of men of state to drive or be driven in a Mercedes-Benz. Mercedes-Benz now offers its newest car, a veritable coupe of state, to the discriminating few who can afford to be seen in this, the finest of machines. It is the new 220 SE coupe with a fuel injection engine, optional power steering and a choice of automatic or four-speed transmission. Its interior is completely hand-fitted with elegant leather and wood embellishments and represents the best of the coachmaker's art. There is no similar car in the world. It combines sports-like performance with the dignity of diplomacy. Further, it carries its silver three-pointed star in the restful silence of complete discretion. That, of course, is entirely in keeping with the seventy-five-year-old tradition of Mercedes-Benz.

Mercedes-Benz Sales, Inc., South Bend, Indiana *(A Subsidiary of Studebaker-Packard Corporation)*

the altimeter is **!** an optional extra **!**

THUNDERBIRD SPORTS ROADSTER. This is the only missile you can inspect without security clearance. With new slipstream headrests and wire wheels, a Sports Roadster looks airborne even when parked. (However, we're forced to admit it really doesn't have an altimeter.) The new assist bar and unique Swing-Away Steering Wheel are practical touches. Versatility's another trait. It's a 2-seater with the tonneau cover on . . . a 4-seater with it off. Ready to solo? Your Ford Dealer has a Sports Roadster—and 3 other lively Thunderbird models—warmed up, and ready for your countdown.

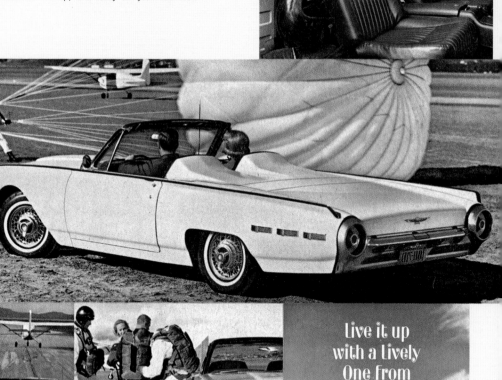

Live it up
with a lively
One from
FORD

A PRODUCT OF
Ford
MOTOR COMPANY

FALCON FAIRLANE GALAXIE THUNDERBIRD

Jaguar elegance: The beauty that's more than skin-deep

Inspect each sweep, each curve, each fluid line of any Jaguar, and you bear witness to Jaguar elegance—a grace of styling that has been engineered from within the heart of the automobile itself. Jaguar elegance is reflected here in two exciting motor cars. One, the new Jaguar XK-E, is available either as an open sports roadster with interchangeable soft or hard top or a completely enclosed *Gran Turismo* coupe. For the family man who requires a roomier vehicle, there is the versatile Jaguar 3.8 Sedan. Pure Jaguar from the word go, this car has been titled "the sedan that behaves like a sports car." Discover Jaguar elegance yourself. See and drive either of these fine Jaguars soon at your local dealer's. JAGUAR CARS INC., 32 East 57th Street, New York 22, N. Y.

Technical Service and Parts Headquarters, 42-50 Twenty-First St., Long Island City 1, N. Y.

Ford, 1962 ◄ *Jaguar, 1962*　　　　　　　　　　　　　　　　　　　　　　　► *Chevrolet, 1962*

Vitality that rides on velvet!

No car anywhere near the price has this one's gift for glove-soft going. Full Coil suspension at all four wheels soaks up shock from the orneriest roads. And a wide choice of power (standard 6 or V8 right up through optional-at-extra-cost V8 mile-shrinkers) lets you trigger your car to your kind of travel. In fact, wouldn't quite a few expensive cars just love to have all the things you get in a spacious and spirited Jet-smooth Chevrolet?

Nudge this baby's "go-pedal" on an open stretch of road and you'll see what Jet-smooth means. Nothing so eager to eat up miles ever went so easy. And so quiet, too, because working with those Full Coil springs are some 700 sound and vibration filters sprinkled liberally throughout the chassis and handsome Body by Fisher. There's plenty more to tempt a traveler, too. Room for roaming with stretchout space to spare. Deep-well trunk that holds odd-size objects and loads at bumper level. Rich appointments a car priced like this never had before. Brainy ideas like parallel-action windshield wipers that clear more glass. The kind of durability Chevrolet's noted for with longer wearing bonded brake linings... long-life zinc- and aluminum-coated muffler... new rust-resisting steel front fender underskirts. What we mean, this one is built for keeps—which is another reason Chevrolet traditionally brings top trade-in over any other full-sized car in its field. Try out a Jet-smooth Chevrolet at your dealer's now. Then just try to be satisfied with anything less.... Chevrolet Division of General Motors, Detroit 2, Michigan.

Jet-smooth CHEVROLET

JET-SMOOTH RIDE

CHEVROLET

Impala Sport Sedan—one of fourteen Jet-smooth Chevrolets to whet your wanderlust!

WHEN YOU FIRST DRIVE UP IN A CADILLAC, *even old friends see*
in a new light. This is going to be especially true when you make your initial entrance in a 1963 Cadillac. A newly refined en
moves the big car so silently you must announce your arrival with a tap of the horn. And when the inevitable inspection co
be prepared for "Ohs" and "Ahs" at the craftsmanship, luxury and elegance of the widest choice of personal options in Cad
history. Isn't there someone you'd like to surprise? Go ahead and do it. Your Cadillac dealer will help you to stage the s

PARDON US WHILE WE SLIP INTO

SOMETHING COMFORTABLE!

INTRODUCING
THE 1963
DODGE

The something comfortable in this case is a 1963 Dodge Polara 4-door hardtop. It's not the clinging sort of comfortable, either; you might say that it's more like housecoat comfortable. Lots of room to move around in. Note the roofline. It sweeps straight back instead of sloping off. It means plenty of headroom for front and rear seat passengers. And everyone rides in more comfort, because Dodge seats are chair-high. All 24 Dodge

models (in three series) offer you this kind of comfort at a variety of prices, all low. Sedans, hardtops, wagons, convertibles — Dependables all. We've got lots for the male side, too. For economy, a going 225 cu. in. 6. For action, a stable full of V8's ranging from the standard 318 cu. in. V8 to an all-out 426 cu. in. high-performance job. There's more: like self-adjusting brakes, 32,000 miles between grease jobs, and a unitized, rust-protected body. The good looks should already be obvious to you. The rest? See your Dodge Dealer.

PICK A SIZE...PICK A PRICE...PICK A DODGE

COMPACT DODGE DART

STANDARD-SIZE DODGE

BIG CUSTOM 880—COMING SOON. ORDER NOW.

Dodge Division of Chrysler Corporation

A FULL LINE OF CARS IN THE LOW-PRICE FIELD !

CADILLAC LADIES LOVE TO PLAY CHAUFFEUR. *Unusual? Not at all.*
*For this one is really fun to drive . . . feather-light and sure to handle . . . smooth and effortless on the move . . . quick
and nimble in the clutches. The reasons are mostly man-talk: a high performance engine, a true center drive line, a triple
braking system, graduated power steering. But the result is eloquent enough for any lady to understand: the finest, sweetest
performance in any automobile today. Visit your dealer soon and see for yourself. And bring your loveliest chauffeur with you.*

Cadillac Motor Car Division • General Motors Corporation

You don't really need Wide-Track . . . unless you drive a car.

Oddly enough, most people don't ride on motorcycles too much, except for fun. And what's fun on a 'cycle isn't fun in a car—namely, leaning 'way over to help get around a turn. That's why we put Wide-Track on Tempest this year: to keep you stable and level when you turn. Tempest isn't the only car with Wide-Track, but we don't fret about the competition. We make the other one too. **Wide-Track Pontiac Tempest**

Exploring inner space

Small spaceman makes big discoveries about Ford interiors

Scene: Ford showroom. While his parents choose their '63 Ford, the astronaut explores. ■ First surprise — Swing-Away steering wheel moves over, ma|

Bright idea — illuminated glove compartment. Spaceman likes bucket seats (will recommend them for school bus). ■ Door lights! Red warns traffic, wh

For major space problems: Ford wagons — most loadspace in low-price field. ■ High-flying compact: Falcon Sprint with tachometer, sporty steering whe

easy (for adults, too). ■ Spaceman inspects console, plush carpeting, sporty floor-mounted shift, crank-vent windows — finds all systems GO (in luxury).

1963

your way in. ■ Space booster: roomy, well lined, illuminated trunk. ■ Fairlane is rated A-O.K. (Note to spaceman's mother: Ford vinyl is soil-resistant).

■ The beautiful exteriors of today's Fords are matched by beautiful interiors. And this beauty isn't just a thin veneer of glamor — it's solid, substantial luxury. ■ Example: Ford's deep-pile carpeting outlasts ordinary car carpeting because it has extra nylon and more loops per square yard. ■ Ford vinyl is heavier, more durable than the vinyl used in other cars. ■ Ford interiors are protected against weather and noise by one-third more insulation than America's other best-selling car. ■ And Fords are designed for comfort. Door openings are higher and wider than other cars in Ford's field . . . passenger space is more than in some medium-price cars. ■ Before you decide on any new car, explore a 1963 Ford — inside and out.

America's liveliest, most care-free cars

FORD

FALCON · FAIRLANE · FORD

ceman's final report to nation: all Ford interiors are . . . out of this world.

over 160 mph...under $5000

Avanti: The Maximum Car. Over 160 mph...under $5,000. No other car—at any price—carries Avanti's record-making supercharged V8...obeys Avanti's racing-type disc brakes...struts Avanti's head-turning aerodynamic shape. Avanti: America's only high-performance 4-passenger luxury car. Apply at your Studebaker dealer's.

From the advanced thinking of

Studebaker
CORPORATION

Ugh.

This is an awful picture of a Volkswagen. It's just not us.

We don't go in much for trading bees or sales jamborees or assorted powwows.

Maybe it's because we don't quite understand the system.

We've never figured out why they run clearance sales on brand new cars.

If there are cars left over every year, why make so many in the first place?

And how come the price goes down, even though the cars are still brand new?

How does the poor guy who bought one last week feel about this week's prices?

Imagine what a problem it must be to keep enough parts on hand when they're always changing. And for the mechanic to keep track of what he's doing.

It's all very confusing.

Either we're way behind the times. Or way ahead.

**About the only thing that can come between
a Corvair owner and his Corvair is**

his wife

'64 Corvair Monza Club C

o with Phillips 66...
e gasoline that won the West!

et to take the family on a big vacation trip? Be
to stop along the way at the sign of Phillips 66.
p with the gasoline that won the West... and
more gallop per gallon. You'll enjoy Phillips
us Western hospitality too—especially if you've

got a Phillips 66 Credit Card. It's good for all Phillips
66 products... and lets you say "charge it" at all Quality Courts Motels! Pick up an application at any
Phillips 66 station or Quality Courts Motel. Go with
Phillips 66—the gasoline that won the West!

PHILLIPS
66

The
Private
World of
Thunderbird

Rambler takes off – the Marlin comes on.
Meet America's first man-size sports-fastback!

You're looking at the most exciting Rambler ever built — Marlin! A car unlike anything else on the scene today. Here's too much automobile to be just another fastback — too much luxury to be just another sport car — too much solid value to be anything but a Rambler. You get dazzling performance, including the might of a 327 cu.-in. V-8 option. You get Power Disc Brakes and individually adjustable reclining front seats, *standard*. You get a choice of practically any sports option you can name, like floor shifts, console, bucket seats, wire-wheel covers — plus *all* the solid extra-value features Rambler provides at no extra cost, such as Deep-Dip rustproofing, Double-Safety Brakes (separate systems, front and rear) — and more. Catch the Marlin in all its excitement — at your Rambler dealer *now*. In limited production, but stepping up fast. American Motors — Dedicated to Excellence

Marlin By Rambler

The ol' lady finally figured out what to do.
A Volkswagen not only holds about twice as much as other station wagons,
but it's economical to keep up, too.
(And the people in the hat next door thought she was crazy.)

Old Volkswagen Station Wagons never die.

The things some people can do with an old box.

But then, he didn't start with any old box. He started with a Volkswagen Station Wagon. Which has about twice the amount of space as an ordinary wagon.

There was room for everything.

A refrigerator, a stove, a table, an instant chili dispenser, and of course, the proverbial kitchen sink.

And a way for it all to get in. The two side doors open into a huge 4' by 4' hole.

Also, its roof may be high compared to other wagons, but its overhead is low. Our Standard VW wagon costs only $2,454.*

However, if you're planning to go into the restaurant business, better not buy one new. (The body's been welded into one solid piece of steel, the tires alone will last for 35,000 miles, and on top of everything else, there are four coats of protective paint.)

It'll take too long to get a new one into bad enough shape.

Strike a blow for originality!
(Take the Mustang Pledge.)

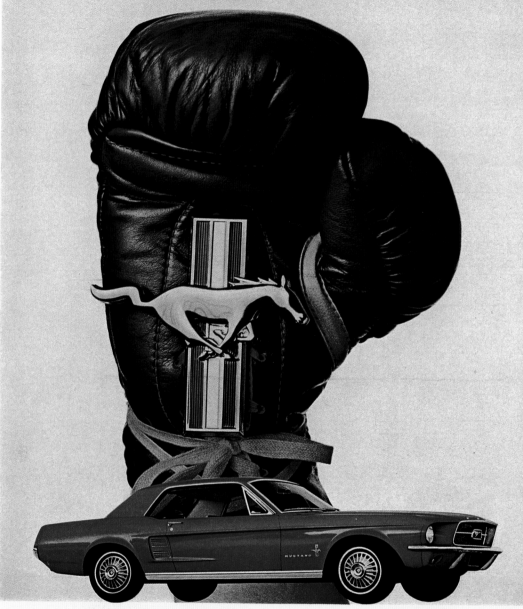

Still the original and lowest-priced car of its kind with bucket seats. MUSTANG

BODY BY FISHER

Who put the living room on the road?

elegant room is "furnished by Fisher." Plush carpeting, luxurious vinyls, bright
ne, deeply cushioned upholstery...even a new reclining bucket seat. And with
d Barrier Silencing, conversation is as easy and intimate as in your own living
. For the pleasures of home, there's no place like Body by Fisher, the only car
known by name. Remember, so much of the buy is in the body. And Body by
r makes a GM car a better buy: Chevrolet, Pontiac, Oldsmobile, Buick, Cadillac.

Body by Fisher

GENERAL MOTORS SYMBOL OF QUALITY

Psssst. Tell your wife it's a family car.

MARLIN '66: Even with buckets* it seats six in comfort. Sizzling fastback power... two 6's, three V-8's
Coil-spring seats and Double-Safety brakes (like Cadillac). See it quick at your friendly Giant-Killer
your American Motors/Rambler Dealer. American Motors... where quality is built in, not added on

*optional

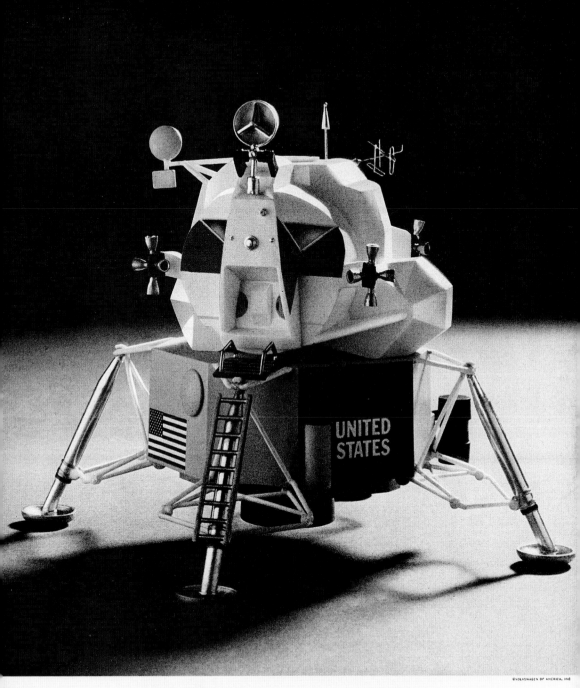

It's ugly, but it gets you there.

The Wizard of Aah's...
new 1966 Fairlane convertible!

1966 Fairlane GT Conv

Now Fairlane swings out with a great new look, an eager new personality, a wide new range of models— including three of the newest convertibles on the road!

You get the idea when you take your first look at the '66 Fairlane GT convertible. Standard equipment includes bucket seats, sporty console, specially sporty GT identification and wheel covers, big 390 cubic-inch V-8, and more. GT has options like GT/A, which means Sportshift Cruise-O-Matic, our new automatic transmission that you can also shift like a manual. Some car! New this year too are an XL convertible, a Squire wagon with Magic Doorgate (swings open like a door for people *and* swings down like a tailgate for cargo!). This year we re-invented Fairlane. Drive one today and see!

Take your pick of a Honda. The Trail 90 left. Or the Rally, one of the Honda Custom Group. These models feature a special type of tank, pipe, handlebars, seat. Ride off on your personalized Honda. Wild.

Honda shapes the world of wheels

You've got to hand it to Honda. New designs. New colors. Altogether 20 models to put a glint in your eye. That famous four-stroke engine takes everything in stride. Won five out of five '66 Grand Prix Championships, 50cc to 500cc. A world's record. With Honda, performance counts as well as style. And that tells it like it is. Any questions? See your local Honda dealer for a safety demonstration ride. **HONDA**

For a free color brochure and safety pamphlet write: American Honda Motor Co., Inc., Dept. QF, Box 50, Gardena, California 90247. ©1967, AHM.

Volkswagen, 1966 ◄◄ *Ford, 1966* ◄ *Honda, 1967*

Business
& Industry
94

Bell-powered Agena satellites in orbit — symbolized.

THE ENGINE WITH THE FUTURE

Reliability . . . Efficiency . . . Flexibility.
In space, these words have a million-dollar meaning.

Vast sums of money and vital scientific data ride on these built-in attributes of Bell Aerosystem's rocket engine for Lockheed's Agena satellite, second stage of the Air Force Discoverer series.

The Agena engine, designed with space in mind long before space became a household word, has fulfilled its every mission and has placed more tons of useful payload into orbit than any other power plant. Its operational reliability is backed by six years of development and 5,000 test firings.

This Bell engine now has re-start capability — the first in the nation. This means that its satellite can change orbit **in space** without the penalty of extra engines. Presently in production, this engine also is adaptable to new fuels and new assignments and, consequently, is programmed for important military and peaceful space ventures of the future.

Agena's engine is typical of the exciting projects in Bell's rocket propulsion center. It is part of the dynamic new approach of a company that's forging ahead in rocketry, avionics and space techniques. These skills serve all government agencies. Engineers and scientists anxious for a new kind of personal challenge can find it at Bell.

BELL AEROSYSTEMS COMPANY
BUFFALO 5, N. Y.
DIVISION OF BELL AEROSPACE CORPORATION
A **textron** COMPANY

General Telephone System, 1960 ◄ *Bell Aerosystems, 1962*

► *Garrett Corporation, 1963*

SOVIET WAY – USA WAY

The difference has made possible (and could save) our very way of life

Stone-surfaced roads, like this, are all there are in many parts of Russia (the known major roads are indicated on the map below). But Russia has a rapidly growing truck "population" (3,000,000 vehicles now, versus 11,000,000 in the U. S.), and a new Soviet seven-year plan calls for building 6,200 miles of superhighway annually through 1965.

Aᴍᴇʀɪᴄᴀ's ᴅɪsᴛʀɪʙᴜᴛɪᴏɴ sʏsᴛᴇᴍ by trucks, over a vast network of highways, is one place where we have a real "competitive edge" over the Soviets.

It's an edge that has had a lot to do with producing our higher standard of living — and could have a lot to do with protecting it.

For instance, American trucks carry nearly 8 times as much freight a year as Soviet trucks.

For instance, there are more than 2,400,000 miles of paved roadway in the U. S. Our Federal superhighway network alone will span some 40,000 miles when completed, and will carry more than 20% of the truck traffic so vital to our national strength.

Best available estimates are that the Soviet Union has fewer than 40,000 miles of paved road altogether, and virtually no superhighways as we know them.

But for all the superiority of our American highways, our trucks are not permitted to take full advantage of all the economies they *could* provide.

This is because of unrealistic limitations on truck sizes and weights that exist in many states. In other states such limitations are more in line with true capacities of the highways, and in these states motor truck transportation is able to operate more efficiently.

Let's take down *all* the artificial barriers. Let's permit motor truck transportation to operate equipment to the full potential capacity of our highways. Let's be sure that America has the advantage of *maximum* efficiency and economy from this vital transportation facility.

Tʜᴇ Wʜɪᴛᴇ Mᴏᴛᴏʀ Cᴏᴍᴘᴀɴʏ
Cʟᴇᴠᴇʟᴀɴᴅ 1, Oʜɪᴏ

Published by
WORLD LEADER IN HEAVY DUTY TRUCKS

WHITE

60 YEARS OF LEADERSHIP

MEMBER
ATA FOUNDATION INC

AMERICAN TRUCKING INDUSTRY
Washington, D. C.

Principal U. S. through-routes alone blanket the map below. And modern trucks, like the one pictured above, provide fast, low-cost freight transportation in America. What's more, America's truck operators are paying 36% of the cost of building our new Federal superhighway network, so vital in maintaining our commanding lead in motor freight.

White Trucks, 1960

ASTRONAUT PROBES SPACE IN A B.F.GOODRICH SUIT

A UNITED STATES PROJECT MERCURY ASTRO-NAUT has become the first American to enter space and return.

From the moment he was sealed in his tiny space craft until he was fished from the Atlantic, he wore a B.F.Goodrich full pressure "space suit".

The fully insulated suit kept the Astronaut at a comfortable 70-odd degrees.

In flight, oxygen was pumped into the suit through a waist connection, circulated about his body to maintain an even temperature, then fed into the helmet for breathing. Exhaled breath escaped through a special vent in his helmet. There was even a communications system built into the suit.

This suit had been custom-fitted to the body of this particular Astronaut. Each of the 1600 separate pieces had been tested under conditions four times greater than those they might be subjected to in use. This is the same type suit that will be worn by U. S. Astronauts in later Project Mercury orbital space flights.

Development of the 20-pound aluminized nylon and rubber suit began in 1934 when BFG designed the pressurized outfit worn by Wiley Post in setting new altitude and speed records. Later the U. S. Navy encouraged B.F.Goodrich to work on a suit that could be worn by fliers at extreme altitudes. It was this Navy suit that BFG adapted, under the guidance and guidance of the National Aeronautics and Space Administration, to today's full pressure suit. This is only a small contribution to the vast total undertaking that has put man into space, but B.F.Goodrich is extremely proud to have been permitted to do its best in behalf of this historic achievement.

Development of the full pressure suit to keep man alive in space is typical of the protection offered by many B.F.Goodrich products. In Korea, troops suffered from crippling frostbite until BFG perfected boots that keep feet warm in sub-zero temperatures. X-ray technicians wear aprons and gloves made of a special BFG material to protect against damaging radiation. And, today, motoring is safer than ever before because the tubeless tire, originated by B.F.Goodrich, provides protection against bruise blowouts. *The B.F.Goodrich Company, Akron 18, Ohio.*

B.F.Goodrich

B.F. Goodrich, 1961

▶ *Douglas, 1960*

How satellites can give us
low cost
emergency telephone service

Launched by the Douglas-built *Thor* IRBM, satellites like this would relay telephone messages anywhere in the world without costly cables or towers.

yond their immediate military cessity, our present rocket and ssile programs promise many al peacetime benefits to us all...

Well past the drawing board stage are ns to use satellites as a low-cost emer-cy stand-by system to relay telephone s around the world.

Your call would be beamed to a satellite, then bounced back to a receiving station on Earth. Cost is estimated at a fraction of what must be spent to install and maintain cables or radio relay towers.

While satellite telephone service is still in the future, *Thor*—the rocket that can put it into being—is thoroughly proved. Built by Douglas, maker of the DC-8 jet-liners, *Thor* has been successful in more than 90% of its shots. It is key booster in the "Discoverer" firings and launched the first nose cone recovered at ICBM range.

Thor is another product of the imagi-nation and experience gained by Douglas in 20 years of missile development.

DOUGLAS

MISSILE AND SPACE SYSTEMS
MILITARY AIRCRAFT • DC-8 JETLINER
TRANSPORT AIRCRAFT • AIRCOMB
GROUND SUPPORT EQUIPMENT

URGENT: Pinpoint a nuclear sub —in thousands of square miles of ocean!

As part of A-NEW, the Navy project to boost equipment effectiveness against elusive nuclear subs, our Sylvania subsidiary is providing an electronic system called the Real World Problem Generator.

The system computer duplicates, in the laboratory, actual tactical situations faced by an antisubmarine warfare aircraft. "Sensed" detection data is presented in the same way that existing and projected electronic ASW gear would sense and display it. In this way the Navy is helped to evaluate its own ASW capability—to find

ways of more effectively using and improving existing equipment—and to develop entirely new ASW devices.

Working with the Navy in the total ASW area is but one way GT&E contributes to our nation's technical advances. The vast capabilities of GT&E, directed by Sylvania Electronic Systems, enable us to handle every phase of almost any kind of electronic system, from initial research to on-location servicing.

Sylvania Electronic Systems, Division of Sylvania Electric Products Inc., 40 Sylvan Road, Waltham 54, Massachusetts.

GT&E
GENERAL TELEPHONE & ELECTRONICS
Total Communications from a single source through

SYLVANIA ELECTRONIC SYSTEMS

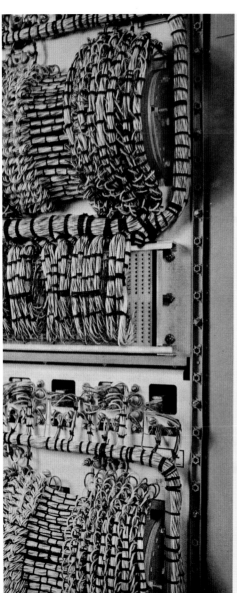

On guard against air attack—The Martin Missile Master
electronic air defense system will protect ten major metropolitan
areas by year's end. First installations have been delivered ahead
of schedule and are now operational. According to the Army,
Missile Master "will provide the most efficient and economical
control and distribution of firepower available for the defense of
strategic areas in the continental United States."

At 00ʰ 00ᵐ 01ˢ GMT, July 1, 1960, Martin logged its 590,304,000th mile of space flight

MARTIN

America's First Family of Rockets and Missiles

AUGUST 1953	MAY 1957	JANUARY 1958	MARCH 1959	MAY 1959	MAY 5, 1961
FIRST successful firing of a large ballistic missile . . . REDSTONE	FIRST successful firing of an intermediate range ballistic missile . . . JUPITER	FIRST satellite . . . Explorer I launched successfully at first attempt and still orbiting . . . JUPITER "C"	FIRST free world solar satellite . . . Pioneer IV first U. S. payload projected to permanent escape from earth . . . JUNO II	FIRST successful space travel and safe return of Primates Able and Baker — JUPITER	First U. S. manned space flight—project Mercury capsule—boosted by the REDSTONE

Chrysler Corporation extends congratulations to all the people who cooperated in the first U. S. manned space flight and in particular, astronaut Navy Commander Alan B. Shepard, Jr.

This flight was boosted by the reliable Redstone—a member of the first team of missiles in America's conquest of space.

This team has established an unequalled record fulfilling missions with reliability and accuracy.

The record is no accident. It is the product of a philosophy of building on proven principles and hardware. The carry-over of experience from the phenomenally reliable Redstone is largely responsible for the equally impressive performance of Jupiter. This inherent integrity is transferred to the succeeding generations of missiles.

There is something else behind this great record. Teamwork — a government-military-industry team working unselfishly in the best interests of the country.

Redstone is operational with U. S. Army forces. Jupiter is deployed by the Air Force. Redstone, Jupiter, Jupiter "C" and Juno II have served the missions of the Department of Defense and the National Aeronautics and Space Administration.

Chrysler Corporation is proud to have been a member of this most successful team since 1952. As prime contractor for the Redstone and Jupiter systems, we have worked closely with military and government scientists in taking these missiles from initial concept to the launching pad . . . and beyond. Broad Chrysler Corporation capability and experience in research, development, engineering, production and logistic support is supplemented by Chrysler operation of the Michigan Ordnance Missile Plant.

Today these missiles mean military strength to keep the peace. They are also the key to the door of a vastly expanded new world of knowledge which will contribute much to peace and a better way of life.

Chrysler Corporation

PLYMOUTH • VALIANT • DODGE • DART • LANCER • CHRYSLER • IMPERIAL • DODGE TRUCKS • MOPAR
REDSTONE • JUPITER • AIRTEMP • AMPLEX • CYCLEWELD • MARINE AND INDUSTRIAL ENGINES

This public information advertisement is paid for by Chrysler Corporation

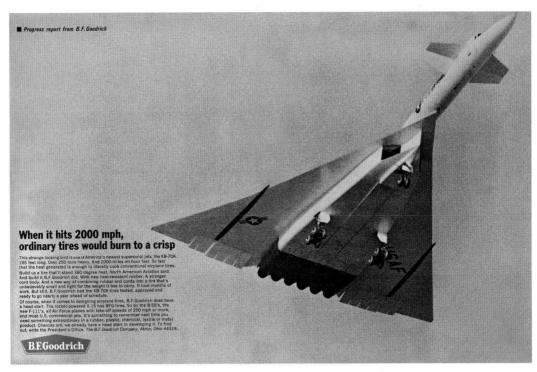

B.F. Goodrich, 1966

Chrysler Corp., 1961 ◀ Chrysler Corp., 1963

When every impression must be letter-perfect... Page after page, carbon after carbon — the work done on your new Underwood Documentor is **electrically** crisp and clear. Here's a typewriter that not only looks smart, it performs brilliantly, too! The high-style Documentor electric is a modern typewriter, from the most complete line of business machines in the world. These office time-savers are the result of Underwood Visioneering—the ability to foresee your particular problem, and help you solve it!

underwood
Underwood Corporation • One Park Ave. • New York 16, N.Y.

Electric, Standard, and Portable Typewriters, Adding and Accounting Machines, Data Processing Systems, Filing Systems, Supplies, Electronic Systems & Components

Underwood, 1960

this is the new IBM Electric

IBM

It's new—inside and out, with 28 engineering achievements that bring you typing at its finest! Your secretary will love its alive, eager response. You'll admire its styling and high-volume output. For this— is the most handsome, efficient typewriter made.

IBM, 1960

Incredible!

Now you can add ✚ subtract ▬ and multiply ✖ electrically at home or office...

for less than $90.00

PRESCRIPTIONS

Use everywhere

At home, office or retail store. This 8 lb. portable is set in its own carrying case—travels anywhere.

SCM

Full-duty electric

...10 keys add, subtract, multiply instantly, total up to 999,999.99. Perfect for office, home or retail store. Saves time—insures accuracy.

New Smith-Corona Figurematic
Made in America

SCM SCM CORPORATION
410 Park Ave., New York 22

Smith-Corona, 1964

ROYAL

"It's so beautiful...so dependable...and you save $95.00"

In simple truth, the $95 saving on every typewriter is only the *third* reason why the new Royal Electress™ is such an extraordinary value among office electrics.

The first reason: This beautiful typewriter produces beautiful results; print work as neat and uniform as a business card.

The second reason: It's a strong, trustworthy typewriter. Its dependability results from new engineering

simplification that eliminates 645 parts in type bar linkages alone. Yet, the Royal Electress is a full-sized electric, with every feature you want and a few found nowhere else.

All this at $95 less than you'd pay for most comparable electrics. Why not let your office staff meet the Electress in person? Your Royal Representative will be happy to demonstrate its advantages. Just call him. He's in the Yellow Pages.

Every year, more Royal typewriters are bought in America than any other brand

Royal, 1969   ▶ Monroe, 1964   ▶▶ Burroughs Corporation, 1964

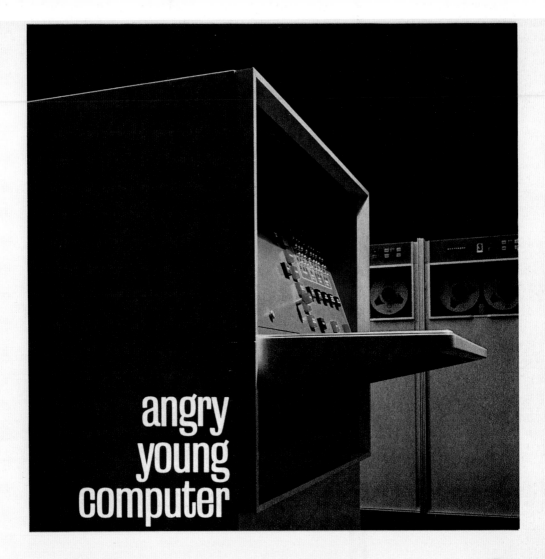

angry
young
computer

Our B 200 can outdo any computer in its class. Any computer,
regardless of name or initials. So
naturally, when it sees a system
being bought or leased on the
<u>basis</u> of name or initials, the
B 200 gets angry. Because it
knows it can do a better job for
fewer dollars. If you know anybody who's considering a computer, do him a favor. Mention
the Burroughs B 200. The same
goes for anybody who's angry at
his present computer. And we
hear a lot of people are. Burroughs—TM

Burroughs Corporation
See a Burroughs computer in action, Election Night, ABC-TV.

Burroughs Corporation, 1963

▶ *Westinghouse, 1964*

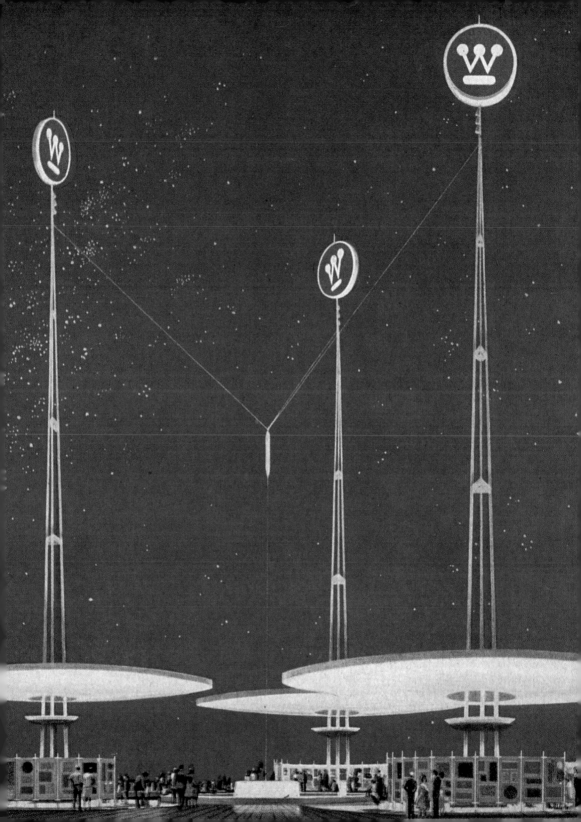

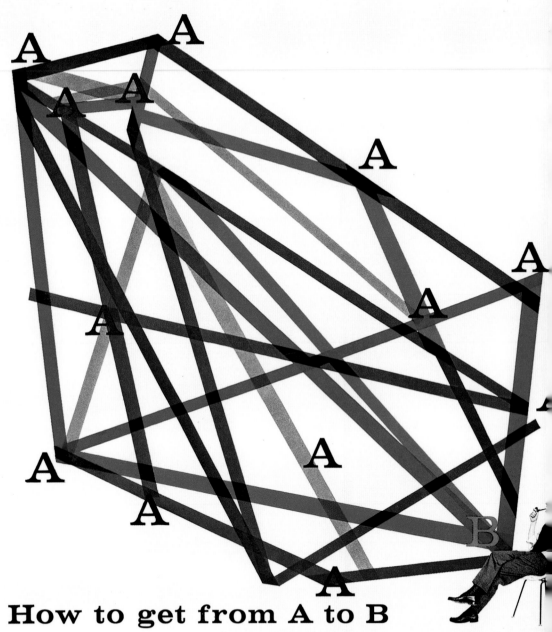

How to get from A to B

This is not a puzzle.

It's a way of keeping electric rates low and making electric service ever more dependable.

You are at B in this symbolic drawing. The A's are the power plants of a number of investor-owned electric light and power companies. The lines show how their power lines connect you with many different plants.

That way, your electricity may be coming from plants run by several companies—some of them hundreds of miles away.

Each company's customers can share in the savings of the newest, most efficient plants. If an emergency shuts down one plant, others can switch their power to its customers.

The investor-owned companies call this

"Interconnecting and Pooling of P

It is one of the many reasons wh companies always have extra powe when America calls for it.

They will continue to do so in the America can plan "growth unlimi homes . . . jobs . . . national strengt power it takes will be waiting—fr investor-owned electric companies

Investor-Owned Electric Light and Power Companies   *Keep America Power*

Sikorsky Aircraft Division of United Aircraft Corporation keeps a 400-year-old idea spinning smoothly with a new product of Shell Research.

Leonardo and some Yankee craftsmen

Leonardo da Vinci had the right idea, but it took Igor Sikorsky and his Connecticut craftsmen to build a workable helicopter.

To perfect it, a rotor had to be devised to cope with an unusual combination of mo-

fore one—and only one—was found: AeroShell® Grease 14. With its use, excessive bearing wear ended and frequent replacement was eliminated.

What's more, this same product more than

in Spain

...and throughout the Free World, some of the most outstanding new process-
industry plants are being designed, engineered and constructed by Lummus

Six Lummus organizations
circle the globe.
Over 50 years of world-wide
experience on over 900 installations
for the process industries.

LUMMUS

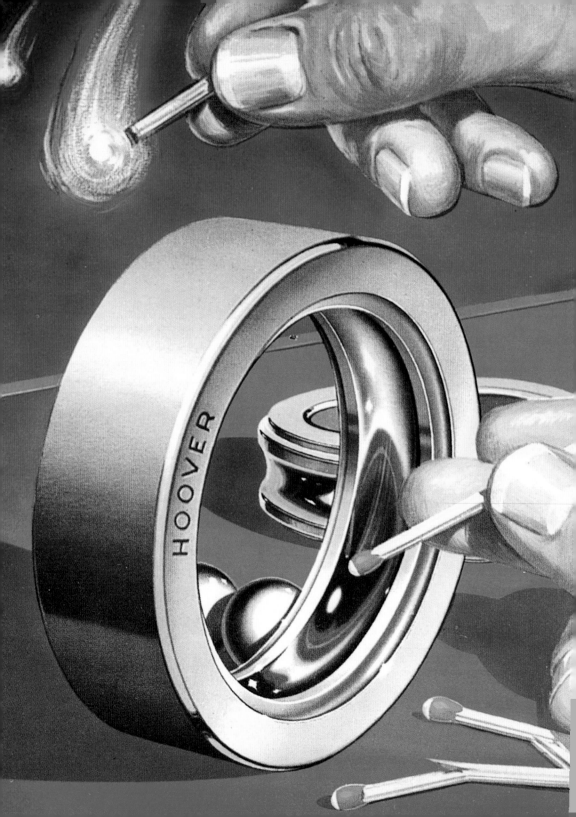

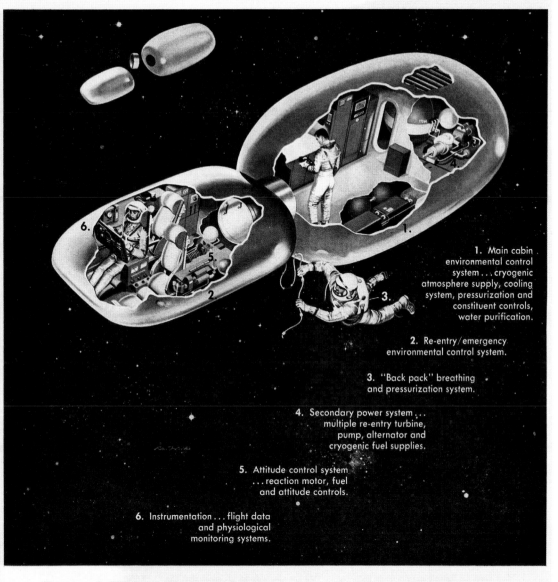

1. Main cabin environmental control system...cryogenic atmosphere supply, cooling system, pressurization and constituent controls, water purification.

2. Re-entry/emergency environmental control system.

3. "Back pack" breathing and pressurization system.

4. Secondary power system... multiple re-entry turbine, pump, alternator and cryogenic fuel supplies.

5. Attitude control system ...reaction motor, fuel and attitude controls.

6. Instrumentation...flight data and physiological monitoring systems.

Successful manned space flight requires reliable and efficient thermal and atmospheric systems and secondary power equipment. Complete and integrated systems, as pictured, are under study at The Garrett Corporation's AiResearch Manufacturing Divisions. Their design reflects 20 years of leadership in airborne and space systems, including NASA's Project Mercury life support system.

Hoover, 1961 ◄

Garrett Corporation, 1960

"*National* Accounting Machines return 200% annually on our investment!"

—HUGHES AIRCRAFT COMPANY, Culver City, Calif.

"Our National System enables us to automatically prepare media for data processing simultaneously with the posting of our inventory records. The cost improvement factors associated with this system have given us a truly economical inventory control operation.

"Our four National Class 32 Accounting Machines save us $46,500 a year, returning 200% annually on our investment.

"We are also pleased to report that the efficiency of our inventory control department has been increased, records are current and accurate, and inventory variances have practically vanished."

C. B. Huestis

C. B. Huestis
Treasurer and Director of Finance
Hughes Aircraft Company

SOME FACTS ABOUT THE GAR-2
AIR-TO-AIR GUIDED MISSILE...
Slightly over six-feet long and six-inches in diameter, this sleek "bird" is automatically launched and unerringly streaks to a bomber kill. Unlike the other models which employed radar as a target-seeking device, the GAR-2 uses infra-red detection to home-in on a target. Just recently the USAF announced that the Super Falcon GAR-3—more deadly than its predecessors—is in production at Hughes' Tucson Plant.

In *any* business, National machines pay for themselves with the money they save, then continue savings as annual profit. Your National man will show how much *you* can save. See Yellow Pages in your phone book.

THE NATIONAL CASH REGISTER COMPANY, DAYTON 9, OHIO
1,039 OFFICES IN 121 COUNTRIES...77 YEARS OF HELPING BUSINESS SAVE MONEY

*TRADE MARK REG. U. S. PAT. OFF.

National

ACCOUNTING MACHINES
ELECTRONIC DATA PROCESSING
ADDING MACHINES · CASH REGISTERS
NCR PAPER (NO CARBON REQUIRED)

"My insurance company? New England Life, of course. Why?"

National Accounting Machines, 1961 ◄ New England Life Insurance, 1969 ▶ Republic Steel, 1960

The indestructible Nauga.

Sadder but wiser mothers pray for permanent furniture. The Nauga answers those prayers. With the hide off his back. Naugahyde vinyl fabric. Naugahyde is so tough, it breaks a kid's spirit. So comfortable, it gets overused. So durable, the kids are old before it is.

With Naugahyde you can sail past the Jones's. It can look like the most expensive   fabrics. Linen. Tweed. Silk. Leather. Wood.

Brocade. Burlap! Bamboo! 500 bewildering varieties and every single one is Naugahyde.

Look for the imaginary Nauga and find beautifully indestructible furniture. His picture is hanging on every piece of real Naugahyde. If you   can't find the Nauga, find another store.

The Nauga is ugly, but his vinyl hide is beautiful.

®Naugahyde is Uniroyal's registered trademark for its vinyl upholstery fabric.

Naugahyde®
vinyl fabric

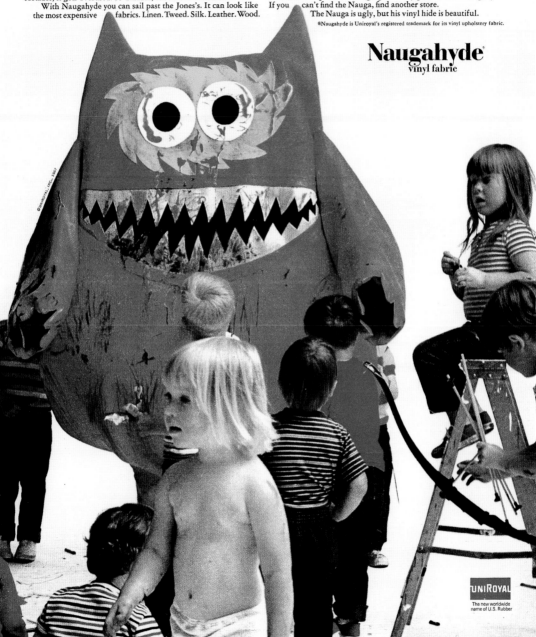

UNIROYAL
The new worldwide
name of U.S. Rubber

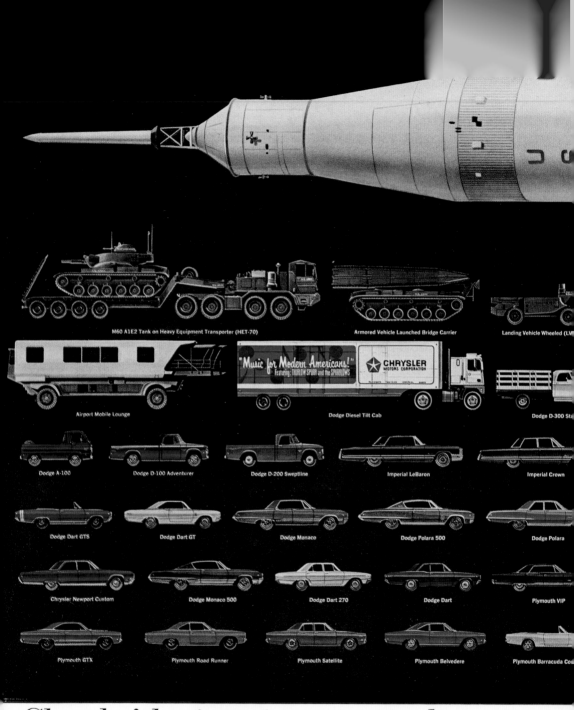

M60 A1E2 Tank on Heavy Equipment Transporter (HET-70)

Armored Vehicle Launched Bridge Carrier

Landing Vehicle Wheeled (LV

Airport Mobile Lounge

"Music for Modern Americans!" Featuring THURLOW SPURR and the SPURRLOWS

CHRYSLER MOTORS CORPORATION

Dodge Diesel Tilt Cab

Dodge D-300 Sta

Dodge A-100

Dodge D-100 Adventurer

Dodge D-200 Sweptline

Imperial LeBaron

Imperial Crown

Dodge Dart GTS

Dodge Dart GT

Dodge Monaco

Dodge Polara 500

Dodge Polara

Chrysler Newport Custom

Dodge Monaco 500

Dodge Dart 270

Dodge Dart

Plymouth VIP

Plymouth GTX

Plymouth Road Runner

Plymouth Satellite

Plymouth Belvedere

Plymouth Barracuda Co

Chrysler's business is to get you where you wa

At Chrysler Corporation, we make things that move.

They splash across lakes. They burrow through marsh mud. They haul pig iron and they haul petunias. They even go so far as to take people out of this world.

You'll find us moving in 130 different countries—with everything from irrigation pumps that move millions of gall water to Airtemp air conditioners that housefuls of cool, clear air.

And the nice thing about Ch

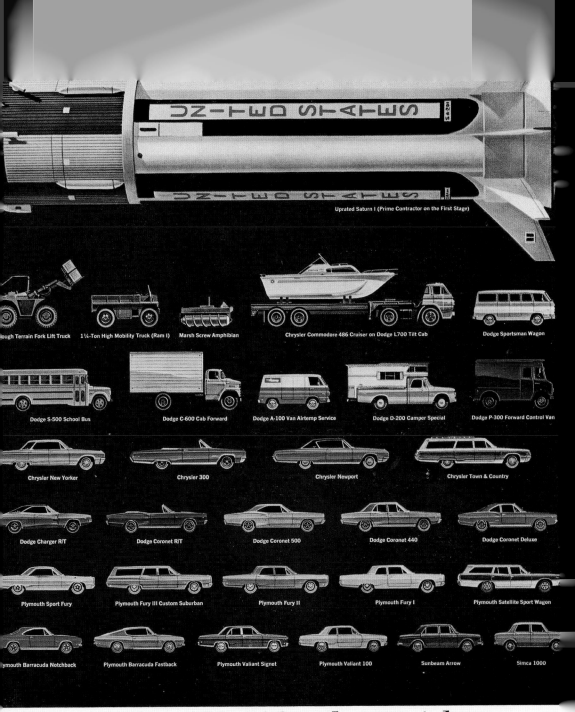

Uprated Saturn I (Prime Contractor on the First Stage)

Rough Terrain Fork Lift Truck   1¼-Ton High Mobility Truck (Ram I)   Marsh Screw Amphibian   Chrysler Commodore 486 Cruiser on Dodge L700 Tilt Cab   Dodge Sportsman Wagon

Dodge S-500 School Bus   Dodge C-600 Cab Forward   Dodge A-100 Van Airtemp Service   Dodge D-200 Camper Special   Dodge P-300 Forward Control Van

Chrysler New Yorker   Chrysler 300   Chrysler Newport   Chrysler Town & Country

Dodge Charger R/T   Dodge Coronet R/T   Dodge Coronet 500   Dodge Coronet 440   Dodge Coronet Deluxe

Plymouth Sport Fury   Plymouth Fury III Custom Suburban   Plymouth Fury II   Plymouth Fury I   Plymouth Satellite Sport Wagon

Plymouth Barracuda Notchback   Plymouth Barracuda Fastback   Plymouth Valiant Signet   Plymouth Valiant 100   Sunbeam Arrow   Simca 1000

go—even if it's 238,000 miles straight up.

...oration engineering is, we also make everything *keeps* moving. Mile after ... Year after year. Maybe that's one rea-... why we've moved up to being the fifth

largest industrial corporation in America.

Plymouth · Dodge · Chrysler · Imperial · Dodge Trucks
Simca · Sunbeam · Airtemp · Cycleweld · Oilite · Mopar
Parts Division · Marine and Industrial Products · Defense
and Space Products · Leasing · Financing · Insurance

CHRYSLER CORPORATION

We're still buildir airplanes around peopl

McDonnell Douglas DC-8s and DC-9s, chosen
more than 60 of the world's leading airlines, w
designed to please the passenger. Now, c
Douglas Aircraft Company is creating new dimensic
in jet travel with the jetliner of the Seventi
the DC-10. The DC-10 will offer unsurpass
levels of comfort and convenience. It continue
tradition of commercial aircraft design, performan
and dependability which has progressed —
without interruption — since 1933.

MCDONNELL DOUGLAS

Picture shows the Yankee Atomic Electric
Plant at Rowe, Mass. operated by a group of
New England investor-owned companies.

ATOMIC ELECTRIC POWER IS HERE
A PEACETIME DREAM COME TRUE...

On this quiet New England river you see just one of the American plants that are now producing electricity from the power of the atom

Operated by the investor-owned electric light and power companies, they form a striking demonstration of America's use of "Atoms for Peace."

Not so long ago it was just science fiction—getting electricity from the power of the atom.

Today atomic power is actually cooking suppers ... running TV sets ... heating, lighting and cooling for many home and business customers of the investor-owned electric light and power companies.

These companies are already operating 5 atomic electric plants. They are spread across the country from New England to California. More are being built.

All over the country, the investor-owned companies carry on research and development on new ways to produce electricity. It is part of their nationwide program to make certain America always has a plentiful supply of power. They can supply all the additional electricity the future will call for.

Investor-Owned Electric Light and Power Companies | *Keep America Powerful*

Company names on request through this magazine

Consumer
Products
128

hold the future in your hand
with **SONY**
RESEARCH MAKES THE DIFFERENCE

THIS IS TELEVISION OF THE FUTURE. This is the personal set predicted for the decade of the Seventies. So light and compact you carry it with you like a book, wherever you go. Put it beside your bed, on your desk at the office, outdoors for picnicking on the patio, in the back of the car or on the boat. It plays anywhere on its own rechargeable battery pack, auto battery or AC, with a picture so bright and sharp ordinary sets pale by comparison. Weighing only 8 lbs., it is hardly larger than a telephone, yet it out-performs standard receivers in sensitivity and durability. Available only in limited quantities, SONY brings it to you today through its advanced research in the epitaxial transistor, so powerful and sensitive it is used only in computers and other advanced electronic equipment —and the new Micro-TV. It would be no exaggeration to say that someday all TV will look like SONY Micro-TV. But why wait for someday? See it today at selected dealers. SONY Micro-TV list $229.95. Optional battery pack.

See and hear the world famous SONY all-transistor, battery operated radios at selected dealers.

SONY CORPORATION OF AMERICA 514 Broadway, New York 12, N.Y.
In Canada: General Distributors Ltd. 791 Notre Dame Ave., Winnipeg.

FRESH FROM MOTOROLA... *new leader in the lively art of electronics*

Old-fashioned reliability comes back in style in modern Motorola® TV

For that spot in your living room where you now have an old TV set that has a genius for conking out during your favorite program, there's a new Motorola that will not only fit in nicely, but also keep giving you a clear, sharp picture until that last ornery cattle rustler gets what's coming to him, and you're ready to call it a night.

Take the TV-Stereo Hi-Fi combination at the left. Your wife will be partial to the beautiful Drexel cabinet (a Motorola exclusive), but you're more likely to appreciate the exclusive Golden Tube Sentry Unit, protecting the tubes against destructive warm-up power surges, main cause of tube failure. That's one reason why Motorola—and only Motorola—guarantees* all tubes and parts on every model for a full year, instead of the usual 90 days.

You can have this famous Motorola reliability in the type and size TV you want (with or without remote control) in a TV-Stereo combination, console, table model or portable. Prices start as low as $139.88**

This country living room, created by Eyvind Earle, achieves an exciting linear pattern through the imaginative use of glass walls, louvered doors, and wooden beams. Motorola's TV-Stereo Hi-Fi combination is taken from Drexel's *Declaration* grouping.

New Motorola Console from Drexel's *Tournier* collection features sliding tambour doors, 23-inch screen (overall diag. meas., 265 sq. in. viewing area), and Golden Satellite® Remote Control.

Ⓜ MOTOROLA

Manufactured in Canada by Eastercast Manufacturing Ltd., license

New Motorola Console with fine-furniture styling.

New Motorola Table TV with 23,000 volts of picture power.

Motorola, 1962

New cabinet design of the Drexel *Tournier* grouping. All Drexel cabinets are the ultimate in fine-furniture craftsmanship . . . fashioned from carefully chosen, beautifully grained hardwoods hand-rubbed to a brilliant luster. Model SK78.

New! Stereo Hi-Fi and Stereo FM with the difference you can hear

If you have an eye for the unusual and an appetite for new experiences, you're probably ready for this latest advance in stereo.

Now that FM is being broadcast stereophonically, (up to now stereo reception has been available only on records) Motorola's three separate amplifiers and three separate speaker systems (instead of the usual two) are more important than ever. You get true stereo effect from a single cabinet . . . and the difference is one you can hear.

In addition, a new and exclusive Motorola development —Vibrasonic—lets you dial new realism into recorded sound . . . in any room, on any record or FM. Sound comes out richer, livelier, more dimensional.

Listen to several different kinds of stereo . . . that's the best way to hear the difference that Motorola's engineering leadership makes.

Motorola will satisfy not only the sensitive ear, but also the discerning eye. There is a wide choice of superb furniture styles, including designs by Drexel.

MOTOROLA Ⓜ

Motorola® Stereo Hi-Fi in Drexel's new *American Treasury* grouping. Drexel models offer Stereo FM optional, extra, and features a new record changer with a feather-true tone arm to make records sound like new, even after a thousand playings. Model SK80.

Motorola, 1963 ◄ *Motorola, 1962*

FRESH FROM MOTOROLA... *new leader in the lively art of electronics*

Styled for people who like in formal living, this Motorola TV-Stereo combination in a compact cabinet less than 45" wide offers as handsome a bit of Early American charm as the eagle on the wall.

Motorola makes it easy to choose the TV that's right for you

If you're shopping for a new TV set here are two good questions to ask yourself: Does it have a dependable chassis? Will it fit in comfortably with the rest of my furniture?

Motorola makes it easy to get an affirmative answer on both counts. In the first place, every Motorola® TV has a hand-wired chassis that's precision crafted for long life with modern hand and dip soldering methods. This extra bit of care has proved so effective that every Motorola TV set carries a full year written guarantee†.

When it comes to selecting a TV set to fit in with your other nice things, Motorola helps you

there, too. You'll see such a wide variety of models and styles, you're almost sure to find the one that's right for you. There are portables as low as $139.88, consoles starting at $229.95; TV-stereo hi-fi combinations from $329.95. All prices shown are manufacturer's suggested list, optional with dealers; slightly higher in some areas.

For TV you can live with happily, see your Motorola dealer. You can choose Early American, Contemporary, or Traditional styling. And many models feature exclusive Motorola cabinetry taken from the luxurious furniture groupings of Drexel and Heritage.

MOTOROLA

For night owls (and people who have to live with them), Motorola TV with a private earphone attachment. Less than $200.00. Radiatbout cart optional, extra.

For do-it-yourself decorators a compact Motorola TV that moves from table, to bench, to stack-on shelf, allows never-ending flexibility in smart room design. $179.95.

For those who like the quiet elegance of neat, trim lines, Motorola TV is fresh, crisp styling that fits in beautifully with Contemporary design. $239.95.

Being "king of the mountain" is a grown-up reality for this young couple. Their contemporary cliff house, hung around a solid rock pinnacle, gives them a commanding view of both the village and the sea below. Point of interest: the Motorola TV-Stereo Hi-Fi combination with FM/AM and FM stereo radio in oiled Walnut cabinetry from the Drexel Declaration grouping.

Motorola, 1963

FRESH FROM MOTOROLA... *new leader in the lively art of electronics*

Dynamic Sound Focus–the latest refinement in Motorola Stereo Hi-Fi

Motorola Stereo Hi-Fi in the elegance and warmth of Drexel's American Treasury styling. Cabinet of genuine Cherrywood veneers and Cherrywood solids. 31" high, 53¼" wide, 18½" deep.

Motorola's Dynamic Sound Focus brings a realism and "presence" to stereo sound that should delight the ear of any audiophile.

This built-in system electro-acoustically sharpens stereo sound reproduction, enabling you to more readily distinguish individual instruments and voices. And because intermixing of sound frequencies in Motorola's three separate amplifiers and three separate speaker systems is minimized, the sound is amazingly crisp, orchestral instruments distinct and sharp. You enjoy experiences and tonal qualities you never thought your stereo records could produce.

The stereo hi-fis pictured here (plus the other models in Motorola's exclusive Drexel-Heritage collection) include Dynamic Sound Focus plus Motorola's Vibrasonic Sound System—the acoustical compensator that adds reflected sound energy to music for live, vibrant sound. These sets also include an FM/AM and FM Stereo radio and Motorola's famous Golden Stereo "1000" Automatic Record Changer.

Make a mental note now to stop by your Motorola dealer's and hear with your own ears the lively difference Dynamic Sound Focus brings to Stereo.

Simple but elegant—stereo hi-fi from Drexel's "Triune styling." Dimensions 30" high, 50½" wide, 18½" deep.

Stereo hi-fi in modern styling. All-wood cabinet of genuine Walnut veneers and select hardwoods. Dimensions: 31¼" high, 53¼" wide, 18½" deep.

Stereo hi-fi is classic French Provincial styling from Drexel's Touraine grouping. Cabinet also available in Custom White French Antique finish.

MOTOROLA

This modern high-rise dwelling makes it possible to "get away" from the city without leaving it. Curved glass window-wall forms panoramic view of the city and surrounding countryside. Reflecting pool and shrubbery add warmth to aluminum room setting, accented by dome ceiling. Motorola's Stereo Hi-Fi is taken from Heritage's Laurente grouping.

Motorola, 1962

FRESH FROM MOTOROLA... *new leader in the lively art of electronics*

A practical guide to successful Santa Clausing

Motorola, 1962

FRESH FROM MOTOROLA... *new leader in the lively art of electronics*

FRESH FROM MOTOROLA... *new leader in the lively art of electronics*

Motorola believes stereo hi-fi should look as good as it sounds

Motorola, 1963

▶ *General Motors, 1968*

Test drive a 1969 Stereo

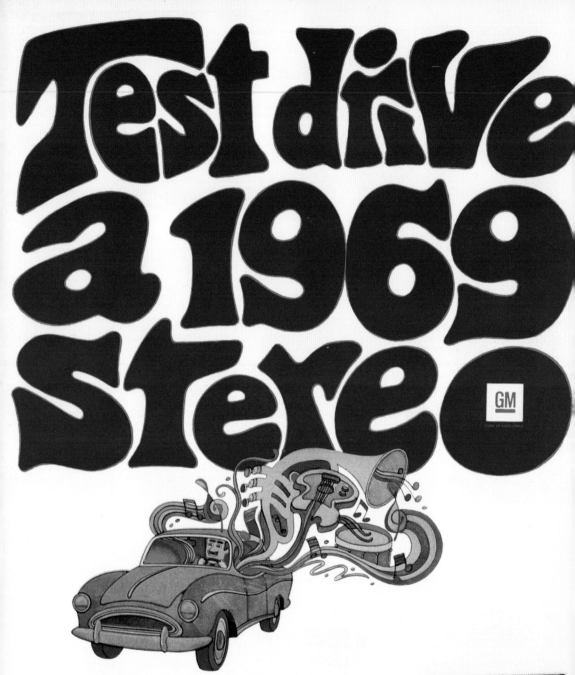

General Motors Delco Car Stereo.

Take it out on a drab day. A rainy day. Right into a sullen traffic jam. Then turn it on.

Suddenly, your world is sunshine! Roses! Bright colors! A world on wheels you never thought possible!

You see, Delco stereo systems are made especially for GM cars. The front-rear speakers are acoustically tailored to each body style to fill your car with a sound that's fantastically rich and real. A sound you can get two ways:

First, with Delco AM/FM Stereo Radio for varied programming.

Or go with the 8-track StereoTape system. Then you can pick a number, any number. And take it with you anywhere.

But you've really got to hear it for yourself. Test drive a Delco Stereo in a new Chevrolet, Pontiac, Oldsmobile, Buick or Cadillac. Ask for one with Delco FM Stereo. Or Delco StereoTape. Or both.

And let the rest of the world dull by.

Delco Radio, Division of General Motors.

SEE "BONANZA" AND MANY OF YOUR FAVORITE SHOWS ON RCA VICTOR "LIVING COLOR" TV

Now, enjoy all the excitement of color in the brightest, most true-to-life RCA Victor Color TV ever...from $399 95 *

optional with dealer

Lifelike natural color. New Vista® Color TV for 1965 gives you the most true-to-life RCA Victor Color ever . . . with better color purity, greater contrast than ever before. Color is so bright, so lifelike, you have to see it to believe it! Crisp, clear black and white pictures, too. Automatic Scene Control for balanced brightness and contrast.

SEE WALT DISNEY'S "WONDERFUL WORLD OF COLOR," SUNDAYS, NBC-TV NETWORK

Most widely proved—dependable. RCA pioneered and developed Color TV—made it a reality—proved it in homes like yours across the country. It's the most widely proved Color TV you can buy. Today, it's America's first choice—more people own RCA Victor than any other TV—black and white or color.

*New low price. Now only $399.95 for the *Darcy*, not shown. Manufacturer's nationally advertised price, optional with dealer. All prices, specifications subject to change.

RCA The Most Trusted Name in Television

Motorola, 1963 ◀ *RCA Victor, 1964*

▶ *RCA Victor, 1967* ▶▶ *Motorola, 1962*

Our new stereo won't add any distortion to their sound. And it won't take any away, either.

When you listen to hard rock, it's not the easiest thing in the world to tell where the sitar ends and the distortion begins. But we at Sony have a new stereo that can help slightly. It's the HP-580.

With it you get FM/AM and FM stereo in the tuner section, 8-inch woofers, 3-inch midranges, and 2-inch tweeters in the speaker section, and a Pickering cartridge in the cartridge section.

It has a Dual 1210 turntable, extremely sensitive FM stereo separation, a high filter switch, loudness control, and specially designed Sony transistors that fit our specially designed electronic circuits. (Niceties you don't usually get from a stereo short of going out and buying components.)

So the Cream won't sound sour. The Strawberry Alarm Clock won't sound piercing.

And because of its built-in dust cover and dustamatic brush, the Rolling Stones will gather no moss.

Nothing-but-the-truth Stereo. The Sony HP580

©1969 Sony Corp. of America. Visit our showroom, 585 Fifth Avenue, New York, N.Y. 10022.

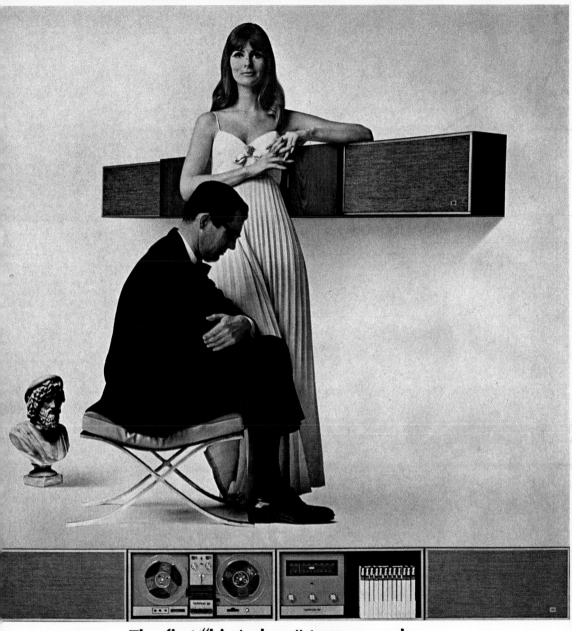

The first "his 'n hers" tape recorder...
new from WOLLENSAK!

This 84-inch wide Wollensak is every inch the man's Tape ~der. Four powerful matched speakers provide true stereo sepa-~ of sound. Solid-state components ensure dependability, instant ~nse. Control Central groups all controls within a handspan. AM-FM ~ tuner and tape storage cabinet. More: twin VU meters, calibrated finger-contoured powered push buttons, self-threading reels.

hers: This is fine furniture — warm and glowing. Fine walnut cabinetry. Speakers faced with textured fabric. Metal surfaces and trim in muted gold tones. Enhances the decor on wall or in bookcase. Matching walnut sliding doors. AM-FM stereo tuner and storage cabinet optional. Model 5800 shown, $299.95*, Model 5300 $279.95*.   *Fair trade prices where law allows.

Wollensak 3M

What you want is a Wollensak

  New twin-wing speaker stereo model 5750

  New compact, model 5710

 New cordless, cartridge portable, model 4100

The new sleek look in superb sound

FOLK ROCK IS A DRAG

hagstrom guitars

You want to knock 'em dea

but not with your breath

use List

Sure, it tastes
Because it's a real germ-killer. On
and you know it works. For hours and

Ensemble by Michael Mott for Paraphernalia

What's a beautiful girl like you doing with a heavy duty detergent like this?

COLD POWER
LAUNDRY
DETERGENT

STOPS DIRT COLD
IN COLD WATER
HEAVY DUTY FORMULA

the whole wash, of course! With new Cold Power, there's nothing to it!
In cold water, new Cold Power coaxes the meanest dirt out of anything London, Paris or
Seventh Avenue can dream up, whether it's a synthetic or natural fabric.
With Cold Power and cold water, there's none of the shrinking, fading, color running or
stain setting you get with hot water. And Cold Power doesn't just take care of your
fashions. It also does the job for everything else you wash. Everything...even slipcovers.
New Cold Power! greatest invention since fashion went washable.

© 1967 Colgate-Palmolive Co.

Listerine, 1969 ◄ *Cold Power Detergent, 1967*

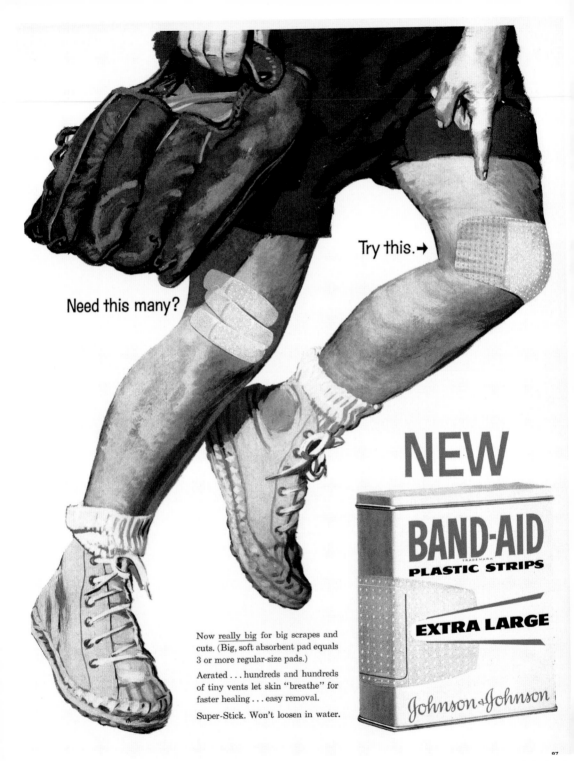

Need this many?

Try this. ➜

NEW
BAND-AID
PLASTIC STRIPS

EXTRA LARGE

Johnson & Johnson

Now really big for big scrapes and cuts. (Big, soft absorbent pad equals 3 or more regular-size pads.)

Aerated . . . hundreds and hundreds of tiny vents let skin "breathe" for faster healing . . . easy removal.

Super-Stick. Won't loosen in water.

Band-Aid, 1960

▶ *Anacin, 1960*

3. Pain

2. Pressure

1. Tension

Lego, the toy they won't be tired of by Dec. 26th

Lego isn't just another empty-minded amusement. It challenges children. To think, to build, to create.

They can turn these colorful plastic bricks into almost anything imaginable: skyscrapers, houses, animals. Simple little things like a flower in a pot. Complicated big things like a truck with moving parts. (Lego even has gear and motor sets.) There's no end to what they can make. And that's what keeps them interested in Lego. Long after most Christmas toys are forgotten.

And when you want to add to a child's Lego collection, give an Extra Parts kit.

Choose from 17 Lego sets —for children 3 to 12. As low as $1.50. 205-piece set shown below, about $5.

Lego...the thoughtful toy.

Samsonite Corporation, Toy Division, Denver.

Lego, 1967

Bring home all the kicks of racing this Christmas with a Revell race set

Revell Rebel "400" Banked Raceway

There's no greater gift for a boy...a car he can race on his own. He'll really race his motor when you bring home a Revell raceway. Especially if he's at that impatient age: Old enough to want a car, but too young to drive one.

He'll get all the thrills of the real thing. He can slam through curves, weave through chicanes, brake hard for turns, go flat out down the straightaway...and really roar around Revell's new banked track! On these steep banked turns, he can hit scale speeds of up to 220 miles an hour. He can race the hot cars, too, like the Mustang 2 + 2, Camaro SS 350,

Ferrari Squalo 555 and Chaparral II. Revell home raceway sets are built to take it...from rugged power packs and controllers, to track that's made to be stepped on. Many have lap counters, so you always know who's winning. All the parts are interchangeable...just keep adding pieces for more and more elaborate layouts. Bring home a Revell. Years from now, he'll still be getting all the kicks of racing at home. So will you. Ten sets to choose from, starting at less than $30.00. Send for free race set catalog to Revell, Inc., 4201 Glencoe Avenue, Venice, California 90292.

Revell

Revell, 1967

SOLD ONLY AT YOUR FAVORITE FOOD MARKET!

"OPERATION X-500"
ROCKET LAUNCHER and DEFENSE BASE

- MISSILES FIRE! • ROCKETS BLAST OFF!
- DIALS LIGHT UP! • CRANE REALLY WORKS!
- NOSE CONES INTERCHANGE! • SCIENTIFIC ACTION TOYS!
- DOZENS OF OTHER WORKING FEATURES!

DEFENSE BASE

ROCKET LAUNCHER

De Luxe
BETTER TOYS FOR YOUNG AMERICA
NEWARK, NEW JERSEY
SUBSIDIARY OF PHILADELPHIA & READING CORP.

Endless hours of fun with the most exciting toy ever made—the super-realistic "OPERATION X-500." Rockets & Missiles soar at the press of a button. Superstructure glides into position to change nose cones. Set includes radar screen, helicopter, space men, scientists, and more! Engineered for perfect safety, easy handling—sure to thrill every child from 3 to 12. Another tremendous value in quality toys by DeLuxe—one of the world's largest toymakers.

COMPLETE SET $11.88

AVAILABLE ON LAY-A-WAY PLAN
RESERVE YOUR TOY NOW!

BRING THIS RESERVATION FORM TO YOUR FOOD MARKET NOW!

PLEASE RESERVE _____ SETS OF OPERATION X-500 by DeLuxe at $11.88 per set

NAME _____

ADDRESS _____

CITY _____

Revell, 1960 ◄ De Luxe, 1960

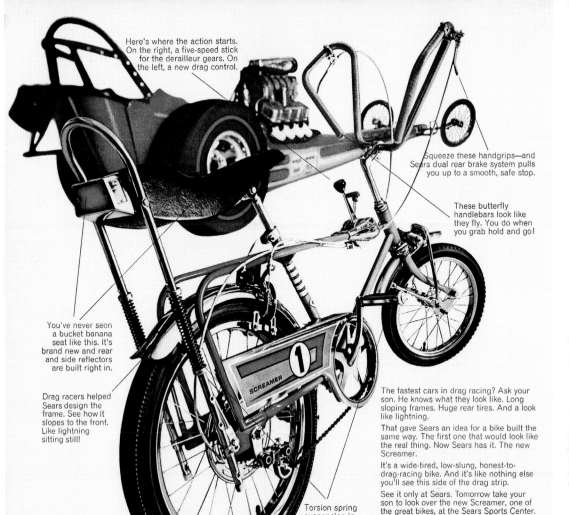

Here's where the action starts. On the right, a five-speed stick for the derailleur gears. On the left, a new drag control.

Squeeze these handgrips—and Sears dual rear brake system pulls you up to a smooth, safe stop.

These butterfly handlebars look like they fly. You do when you grab hold and go!

You've never seen a bucket banana seat like this. It's brand new and rear and side reflectors are built right in.

Drag racers helped Sears design the frame. See how it slopes to the front. Like lightning sitting still!

Torsion spring suspension in front and dual coil-spring shocks in back smooth out the bumps of the roughest roads.

The fastest cars in drag racing? Ask your son. He knows what they look like. Long sloping frames. Huge rear tires. And a look like lightning.

That gave Sears an idea for a bike built the same way. The first one that would look like the real thing. Now Sears has it. The new Screamer.

It's a wide-tired, low-slung, honest-to-drag-racing bike. And it's like nothing else you'll see this side of the drag strip.

See it only at Sears. Tomorrow take your son to look over the new Screamer, one of the great bikes, at the Sears Sports Center. Or look in the Sears, Roebuck and Co. Catalog.

Sears ◉
SPORTS CENTER
where the new ideas are

Sears wheels out the first bike with a frame like a drag racer.

How your kids can have a happier Halloween

Boo! The trick is to treat them to transparent "Scotch" Brand Tape . . . to make a mask, a witch's hat, a magic wand—even create the entire costume with crepe paper and tape. Or to play *tape*-the-tail-on-the-cat (no dangerous pins!). Grownups can help: tape penny candy in wax paper for treating callers —tape paper pumpkins, fall leaves, scary things to windows and mirrors for a true Halloween look. The other 364 days, too, "Scotch" Brand Tape is sharp as a witch's wand at making fun come true. Keep it handy all year 'round for the kids—and for *you!*

3M MINNESOTA MINING & MANUFACTURING CO.

© 1961 3M Co., St. Paul 6, Minn.   . . .WHERE RESEARCH IS THE KEY TO TOMORROW

When tape costs so little, why settle for less than the best— "Scotch" Brand in the plaid dispenser

Next time, buy two—one for the kids and one for you!

Huge "Happiness" Offer from Helms!

FROM YOUR SNAPSHOT...

TO THIS FULL-COLOR PORTRAIT...

RENDERED IN OIL PASTELS BY AMERICAN ARTISTS

LIFE-SIZE FRAMED OIL-PASTEL PORTRAIT

BEAUTIFULLY FRAMED FULL-COLOR PORTRAIT FROM YOUR FAVORITE SNAPSHOT!
ORDER IT—AND DELICIOUS HELMS BREAD—AT YOUR DOOR FROM YOUR HELMSMAN...NOW!

ONLY **$9⁹⁵** COMPLETE
PLUS FIVE (5) HELMS BREAD WRAPPERS

Imagine ... a life-size, full-color oil pastel portrait by fine American artists to your guaranteed* satisfaction from your favorite color or black & white snapshot... and

*In writing

HELMS BAKERIES

framed in a beautiful 15″ x 19″ carved Gold and Antique White frame...ALL FOR $9.95 COMPLETE, PLUS 5 HELMS BREAD WRAPPERS!

HERE'S ALL YOU DO...
(1) Enjoy the superb flavor and freshness of your favorite Helms Bread. (2) Give your snapshot, 5 Helms Bread wrappers

and $9.95 to your Helmsman. He will personally deliver your completed, framed portrait to your door—and return your snapshot—within 30 days!

ACT NOW...don't miss this once-in-a-lifetime offer! Order as many as you like ...these magnificent portraits make memorable, lasting gifts.

(Offer expires December 15, 1967).

HELMS HOME-DELIVERS HAPPINESS

Kal Kan Dog Food, 1963 ◀ *Helms Bakery, 1967*

162 Consumer Products

FUTURE HOMES will be able to face in any direction — turned at will by your electricity. Electrically operated climate-conditioned extensions will permit "summer terraces" all year round — enjoy winter and summer fun both at once.

Power companies doubling electricity for new kind of living

Plenty of electricity can make your home of the future a house of marvels!

To help bring this new electric age, America's more than 400 independent electric light and power companies are *doubling* today's electric supply — building power plants and lines at a rate of $2 billion a year.

In the future, you'll be able to flip switches to raise or lower table and work surfaces to any height. Electricity will bring beds out of the walls in the evening — then "make" them and fold them into the walls in the morning. The power that controls your home's climate will even do the dusting.

You'll need much more electricity, and you'll get it — from America's independent electric companies. And unlike federal electric systems, these companies don't depend on tax money to build for your future.

In the new electric age — as always — people will benefit most when served by companies like the ones bringing this message — *America's Independent Electric Light and Power Companies**.

America's Independent Electric Light and Power Companies

▶ *Great Books, 1965*   ▶ ▶ *World Book Encyclopedia, 1961*

Why the Godless hate these books

...and why the God-fearing find daily inspiration in them

Great Books contain the great truths that are fatal to dictators, vital to religious men and women everywhere. In these volumes you can trace the origin and development of religious freedom, tolerance, the brotherhood of man, and other concepts by which you live.

From the pages of Great Books, 74 immortal authors speak to you. From them you can gain strength to live with the troubles of our times.

As you read them your mind is stimulated, your spirits lifted, your life enriched. You see why these great thoughts are the deadliest enemies of tyrants. No one can combat these truths except by denying men the right to know them.

What kinds of men wrote Great Books?

Were they all Christians? No. Some of them—Homer, Aeschylus, Aristotle and others—lived and died before Christ was born.

Were they all religious writers? Augustine was, but not Shakespeare. Thomas Aquinas was, but not Thomas Jefferson.

Yet these 74 immortals, whose numbers include poets, philosophers, dramatists, novelists, historians, scientists, political and economic thinkers, are all important to the church-going millions of Americans today.

Their ideas—443 works, combined *only* in the 54 superbly bound volumes of Great Books—are the foundation of our free institutions.

The amazing Syntopicon

With Great Books you receive the two-volume Syntopicon, a unique idea index that enables you to trace every thought in Great Books *and in the Bible*, as easily as you look up words in your dictionary.

For example, suppose you wish to compare Plato's ideas on life after death with the teachings of the Bible. In the Syntopicon under "Immortality," you find chapter-and-verse references to *all* mentions of the subject in the Bible, *plus* exact references to each of the hundreds of ideas on immortality in Great Books.

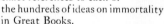

FREE OFFER ... act now!

Find out more about Great Books. Just mail in the attached post card for a profusely illustrated 16-page booklet—*free*. Send for it today—no postage required. Great Books, Dept. 339-I, 425 No. Michigan Ave., Chicago, Illinois 60611.

GREAT BOOKS

Some people even *United* can't help!

If you can pack your possessions on the back of a bike, you won't have much use for our services. Not that we have anything against people traveling light. It's just that United's "Pre-Planned" moving service was meant for families who have everything ... including the big problem of getting it all safely to a new home.

We've added special wrinkles like Sanitized* vans to keep a family's possessions fresh and clean. We've taught our packers to treat each fragile item like an heirloom when they place it in our custom built containers. And we've made "new city" information free and easy to get through our Bette Malone Moving Consultant Service. So even though we can't be of immediate service, we hope you'll keep us in mind. We're easy to find in the Yellow Pages under "MOVERS."

Serving the United States, Canada and 114 Foreign Lands

UNITED MOVES THE PEOPLE WHO MOVE THE WORLD!

United Van Lines

*Reg. U.S. Pat. Off.

Hallmark, 1961 ◄ *United Van Lines, 1969*

► *Dennison, 1962* ►► *Cannon, 1969*

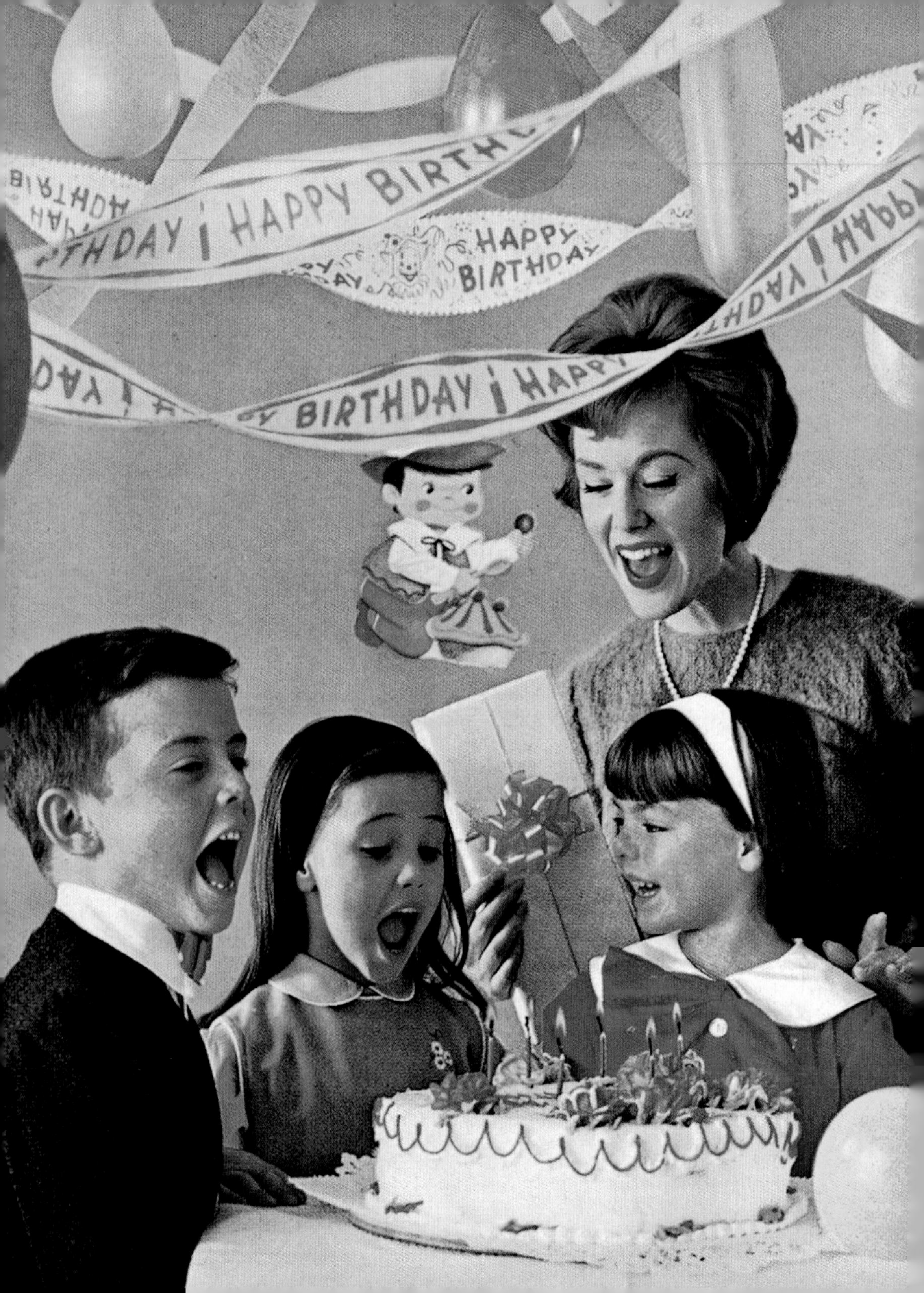
HAPPY BIRTHDAY
HAPPY BIRTHDAY
BIRTHDAY HAPPY

Homeroom.

This is the place.
A place you can decorate all by yourself.
With crispy no-iron sheets that match
fringed bedspreads and fluffy towels.
Cannon Royal Family makes stuff like that
And Cannon would like a place in your place.
So why don't you look us up
the next time you're in town.

CANNON
ROYAL FAMILY

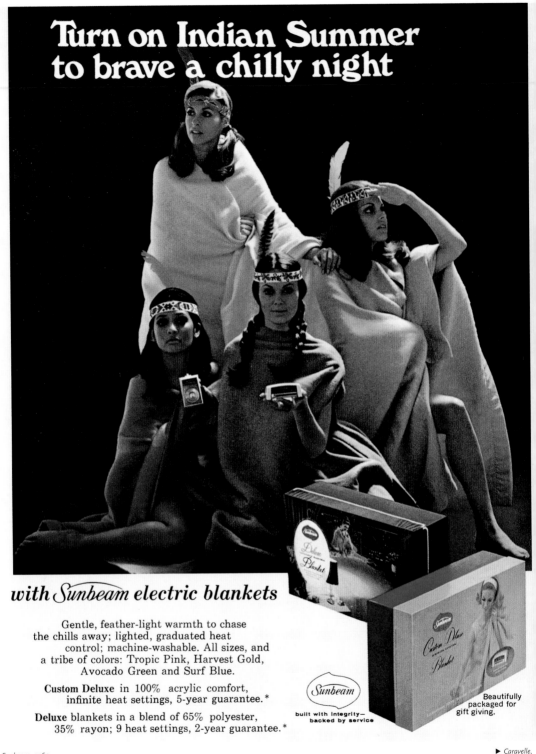

Turn on Indian Summer to brave a chilly night

with *Sunbeam* electric blankets

Gentle, feather-light warmth to chase
the chills away; lighted, graduated heat
control; machine-washable. All sizes, and
a tribe of colors: Tropic Pink, Harvest Gold,
Avocado Green and Surf Blue.

Custom Deluxe in 100% acrylic comfort,
infinite heat settings, 5-year guarantee.*

Deluxe blankets in a blend of 65% polyester,
35% rayon; 9 heat settings, 2-year guarantee.*

Sunbeam

**built with integrity—
backed by service**

Beautifully
packaged for
gift giving.

Sunbeam, 1969

▶ *Caravelle,*

COLOR, EVERYONE?

Sure, but which? Here they are: nine of the glowing colors you may select in the handsome new phones Western Electric makes for Bell telephone companies. The picture chart above shows the relative public popularity of these telephone colors. Have you seen them lately at your Bell business office?

The trend in telephones is definitely to color—in both home and office —to complement any decor, or just for the sheer fun of it. And we at

Western Electric are happy to oblige; in fact, *two-thirds* of all new telephones we'll make this year will be in color. The rest will be in traditional black.

Producing good looking, dependable telephones and the equip- needed to serve you, is one of our main jobs as part of the Bell Sys-

Western Electric **manufacturing and supply unit of the Bell Sys-**

Western Electric
is crossing a telephone with a TV set.

Someday you'll be a star!

What you'll use is called, simply enough, a Picturephone® set. Someday it will let you see who you are talking to, and let them see you.

The Picturephone set is just one of the communications of the future Western Electric is working on with Bell Telephone Laboratories.

Western Electric builds regular phones and equipment for your Bell telephone company. But we also build for the future.

Western Electric
MANUFACTURING & SUPPLY UNIT OF THE BELL SYSTEM

Western Electric, 1960 ◄   *Western Electric, 1968*   ► *Motorola, 1963*

Now Schick has invented the world's fastest home hairdryer!
(so relax and enjoy it)

©1962 Schick, Inc., Lancaster, Pa./Schick (Canada) Limited, Toronto, 28

Hair wet, or just set? Get into something comfortable—the new Schick Petite Salon Home Hairdryer. The heat is smooth and even—never a "hot spot." The bouffant hood fits over your largest rollers. It's the fastest—and quietest—of all home hairdryers! Cuts drying time to next-to-nothing!

Travels light, too. For speed, comfort and ease, there's nothing like the new Schick Petite Salon ..... so relax—and enjoy it!

SCHICK
Ⓢ *the mark of quality*

NEW SCHICK *Petite Salon* HAIRDRYER
For the finest quality in ladies' electric shavers, look for the Crown Jewel by Schick.

Schick Hairdryer, 1962

▶ *Schick Hairdryer, 1963*

Just like drying your hair in the fresh desert air!

AT HOME FASHION BY PERFECT NEGLIGEE

The new Schick *Le Salon* professional hairdryer
especially designed for home use
(gives you the ultimate in speed and comfort!)

Salon by Schick dries your hair <u>faster</u>, <u>better</u> than any other you've ever used. Its <u>soft</u>, phyr-like <u>air</u> flows from tiny holes in the roomy hood...air so <u>gentle</u> you never need a. And so comfortable! With Le Salon you can forget about covering your ears or ck. No nerve-wracking noise either. And so <u>safe</u> to use—<u>doesn't</u> change the color of ached or tinted hair the way other hairdryers can. (Perfect children's hair, too!) With Le Salon, you have easy-to-adjust perature control. And you'll love how it fits into any decor, ves easily on its own wheels, stores in the smallest space.

SCHICK
Ⓢ *the mark of quality*

Fastest portable Hairdryer...ever!

SCHICK PETITE SALON
WITH TRAVEL CASE,
built-in mirror and
manicure center,
bouffant hood.

Wing Orchard Posters, 1968

▶ *General Electric, 1969*

AMAZING $2 OFFER!

GIANT 24"x36" (peter max)
Psychedelic Posters

Peter Max

DONOVAN

PRANA

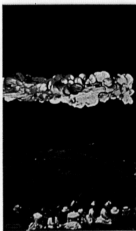

PSYCHEDELIC CLOUD

W. C. FIELDS

CAPTAIN MIDNIGHT

TOULOUSE LAUTREC

Never before in the history of psychedelic art has such a fabulous collection made the scene! From the head of Peter Max, the Master of them all, these six, 4-color posters capture the full meaning of this fascinating form of cosmic art expression. But you cannot appreciate the full rich Dayglo colors from the small pictures above— the only real thrill is by owning them. So take your choice of all of them: DONOVAN, PRANA, PSYCHEDELIC CLOUD, W. C. FIELDS, CAPTAIN MID-NIGHT and TOULOUSE LAUTREC.

OFFER MAY NOT BE REPEATED THIS SEASON

We urge you to order your full color reproductions now while the supply lasts. We will send each to you for just $2 plus 10¢ postage. Each of these fine art posters is 24" x 36" and great to look at under strobe lights while digging your music. This may be your only chance to order.

Eye Magazine, 1968

► *Capitol Records, 1968*

FROM WHERE IT'S HAPPENING!
20 OF THE FREAKIEST POSTERS EVER!
FAMILY DOG PRODUCTIONS' ORIGINALS
For One Of San Francisco's Most *Psychedelic* Ballrooms!
At Your Favorite Record Dealer-$1 Apiece! *

*OPTIONAL WITH DEALER

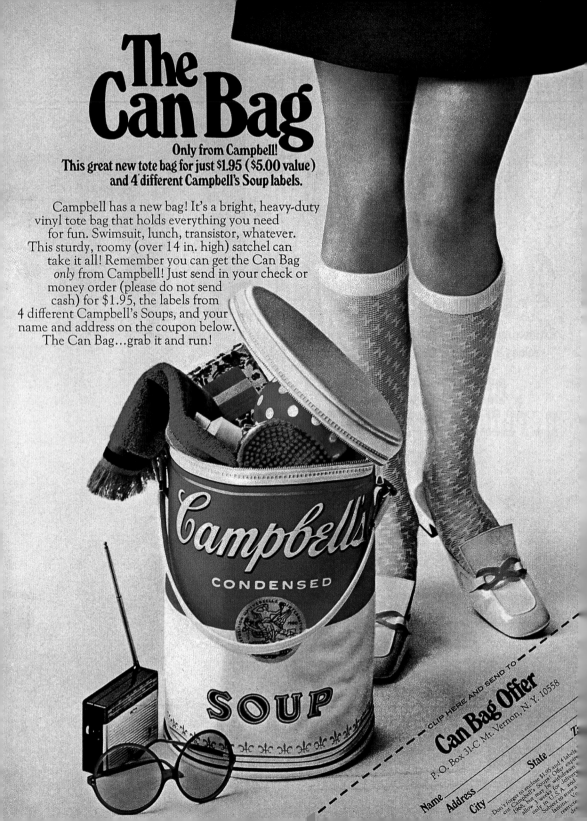

The Can Bag

Only from Campbell!
**This great new tote bag for just $1.95 ($5.00 value)
and 4 different Campbell's Soup labels.**

Campbell has a new bag! It's a bright, heavy-duty vinyl tote bag that holds everything you need for fun. Swimsuit, lunch, transistor, whatever. This sturdy, roomy (over 14 in. high) satchel can take it all! Remember you can get the Can Bag *only* from Campbell! Just send in your check or money order (please do not send cash) for $1.95, the labels from 4 different Campbell's Soups, and your name and address on the coupon below. The Can Bag...grab it and run!

Campbell's
CONDENSED

SOUP

Campbell hits the beach!

When it's time to toss in the towel (into the beach bag, that is) — *this* is the towel to toss in! It's a mad, mad all-cotton beach towel that measures a big 34" x 62" of thirsty terry, wildly printed with a giant-size Campbell's Soup can. A $3.95 retail value that you can snatch up for just $1.95 plus 4 different labels from Campbell's Soup cans. It's a big bargain, a big towel, and a big howl on the beach when you spread it out! A guaranteed conversation-starter, sure to attract crowds and crowds of devastatingly attractive males! Send for yours and hit the beach BIG this year!

Get a Campbell Towel for only $1.95 plus 4 labels!

Yes, I want to toss in the towel! Send me _____ Campbell Towel(s). For each one ordered I enclose $1.95 plus 4 Campbell's Soup labels. (You realize, of course, that you're all wet if you don't order more than one! They make great gifties for good friends!)

To: Beach Towel Offer, P.O. Box 4260, Clinton, Iowa 52732

Name

Address

City   State   Zip

Campbell's Soup, 1969 ◄   *Campbell's Soup, 1968*

Enter–
tainment
184

Barbarella, 1968 ◀◀ *When Dinosaurs Ruled The Earth, 1969* ◀   *What A Way To Go!, 1964*   ▶ *2001 A Space Odyssey, 1968* ▶▶ *The Impossible Years, 1968*

187

An epic drama of adventure and exploration!
World Premiere April 2nd

YOU VISIT SPACE STATION ONE: The First Step In An Odyssey That Will Take You To The Stars And Beyond.

MGM PRESENTS A STANLEY KUBRICK PRODUCTION

2001: a space odyssey

CINERAMA®

STARRING
KEIR DULLEA · GARY LOCKWOOD

SCREENPLAY BY
STANLEY KUBRICK AND ARTHUR C. CLARKE

PRODUCED AND DIRECTED BY
STANLEY KUBRICK

SUPER PANAVISION® AND METROCOLOR

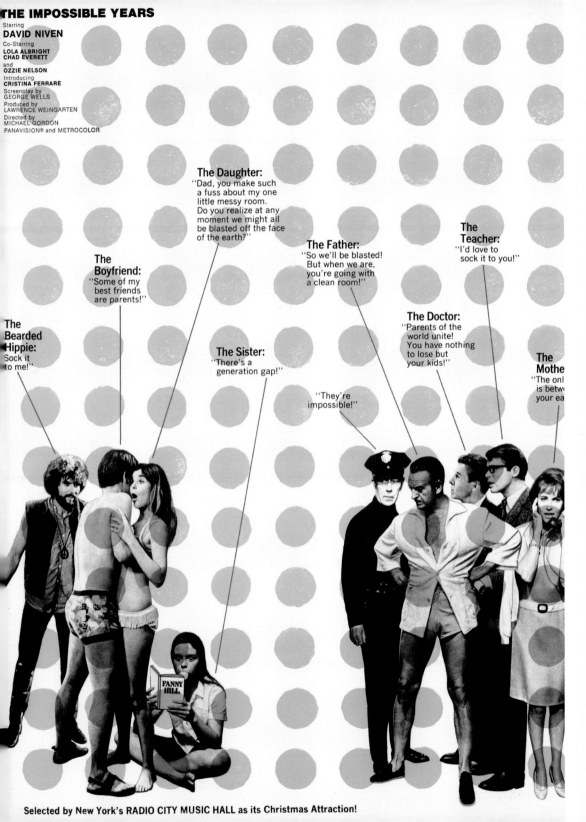

THE IMPOSSIBLE YEARS

Starring
DAVID NIVEN
Co-Starring
LOLA ALBRIGHT
CHAD EVERETT
and
OZZIE NELSON
Introducing
CRISTINA FERRARE
Screenplay by
GEORGE WELLS
Produced by
LAWRENCE WEINGARTEN
Directed by
MICHAEL GORDON
PANAVISION® and METROCOLOR

The Daughter:
"Dad, you make such
a fuss about my one
little messy room.
Do you realize at any
moment we might all
be blasted off the face
of the earth?"

The Teacher:
"I'd love to
sock it to you!"

The Father:
"So we'll be blasted!
But when we are,
you're going with
a clean room!"

The Boyfriend:
"Some of my
best friends
are parents!"

The Doctor:
"Parents of the
world unite!
You have nothing
to lose but
your kids!"

The Bearded Hippie:
"Sock it to me!"

The Sister:
"There's a
generation gap!"

The Mothe
"The onl
is betwe
your ea

"They're
impossible!"

FANNY
HILL

Selected by New York's RADIO CITY MUSIC HALL as its Christmas Attraction!

JERRY LEWIS BRINGS A THOUSAND YEARS OF STORY-TELLING

FUN TO SPARKLING NEW LIFE ON THE SCREEN

AS

Cinderfella

(A Jerry Lewis Production)

Norman Rockwell

You're going to have a magic movie ball! Jerry as the poor fella kicked around by his nasty stepmother and stepbrothers— who goes all aglow at the Princess' dance — just before midnight!

co-starring

ED WYNN · JUDITH ANDERSON · HENRY SILVA · ROBERT HUTTON

with COUNT BASIE and his World Renowned Band featuring Joe Williams

and

ANNA MARIA ALBERGHETTI as "The Princess"

Produced by Jerry Lewis · Associate Producer – Ernest D. Glucksman · Written and Directed by Frank Tashlin
Musical Numbers Staged by Nick Castle · New Songs by Harry Warren and Jack Brooks · A Paramount Release

TECHNICOLOR

FOR THE HOLIDAY SEASON—AT YOUR FAVORITE MOTION PICTURE THEATRE!

The Greatest Adventure Ever Lived Becomes The Greatest Adventure Ever Filmed!

METRO-GOLDWYN-MAYER presents

MARLON BRANDO
as Fletcher Christian

TREVOR HOWARD
as Captain Bligh

RICHARD HARRIS
as John Mills

IN

AN AARON ROSENBERG PRODUCTION

MUTINY ON THE BOUNTY

CO-STARRING
HUGH GRIFFITH · RICHARD HAYDN
WITH
and TARITA · PERCY HERBERT
SCREEN PLAY BY   DIRECTED BY
CHARLES LEDERER · LEWIS MILESTONE
Based on the Novel by CHARLES NORDHOFF and JAMES NORMAN HALL
MUSIC BY BRONISLAU KAPER
FILMED IN ULTRA PANAVISION 70® · TECHNIRAMA®

MUTINY ON THE BOUNTY NOW PLAYING, OR SOON TO OPEN, IN THESE CITIES

ATLANTA ROXY • BALTIMORE TOWNE • BOSTON SAXON • BUFFALO TECK • CHICAGO CINESTAGE • CINCINNATI VALLEY CLEVELAND LOEW'S OHIO • COLUMBUS, O. CINESTAGE • DALLAS TOWER • DAYTON McCOOK • DENVER DENHAM DETROIT UNITED ARTISTS • HOUSTON TOWER • INDIANAPOLIS LYRIC • KANSAS CITY CAPRI • LONDON ROYALTY LOS ANGELES EGYPTIAN • LOUISVILLE BROWN • MIAMI BEACH SHERIDAN • MILWAUKEE STRAND • MINNEAPOLIS ACADEMY MONTREAL ALOUETTE • NEW YORK CITY LOEW'S STATE • OMAHA COOPER • PHILADELPHIA STANLEY • PHOENIX VISTA PITTSBURGH NIXON • PORTLAND, ORE. MUSIC BOX • SALT LAKE CITY CENTRE • SAN FRANCISCO CORONET • SEATTLE BLUE MOUSE • ST. LOUIS ESQUIRE • ST. PETERSBURG CENTRE • TORONTO UNIVERSITY • VANCOUVER, B.C. STANLEY WASHINGTON, D.C. WARNER / *Watch your local newspaper for the "Mutiny on the Bounty" engagement in your city.*

Hatari, 1962 ◄◄ *Cinderfella, 1960* ◄ *Mutiny On The Bounty, 1962*

THE SPY WHO CAME OUT OF THE WATER

She's the drip-dry spy
licensed for laughs
with the craziest cast
in the funniest
undercover plot
of the year!

METRO-GOLDWYN-MAYER
PRESENTS
A MARTIN MELCHER-
EVERETT FREEMAN PRODUCTION

STARRING
DORIS **ROD** **ARTHUR**
DAY **TAYLOR** **GODFREY**

CO-STARRING
JOHN McGIVER · PAUL LYNDE · EDWARD ANDREWS · ERIC FLEMING
DOM DE LUISE and DICK MARTIN as "Zack" · EVERETT FREEMAN
DIRECTED BY   PRODUCED BY
FRANK TASHLIN · MARTIN MELCHER and EVERETT FREEMAN
IN **PANAVISION** AND **METROCOLOR**

The Glass Bottom Boat

Watch for it at a theatre
near you this summer!

The Glass Bottom Boat, 1966

Hey Big Spender, spend a little time with

SWEET CHARITY

"It is gorgeous, it is exciting,
it is stimulating,
it is breathtaking."

United Press International

SWEET CHARITY · **SHIRLEY MacLAINE**

co-starring JOHN McMARTIN · CHITA RIVERA · PAULA KELLY · STUBBY KAYE and RICARDO MONTALBAN as The Actor

STARRING

and SAMMY DAVIS, JR. as Big Daddy · Screenplay by PETER STONE · Directed and Choreographed by BOB FOSSE

Produced by ROBERT ARTHUR · From the New York Stage production · Book by NEIL SIMON · Music by CY COLEMAN · Lyrics by DOROTHY FIELDS · Staging and Choreography by BOB FOSSE

Based upon an original screenplay by FEDERICO FELLINI, TULLIO PINELLI and ENNIO FLAIANO · Produced by FRYER, CARR & HARRIS

A UNIVERSAL PICTURE · TECHNICOLOR® 70MM · PANAVISION® WITH FULL DIMENSIONAL SOUND

Original sound
track album
now available
exclusively on
Decca Records
and Decca 4 and
8 track cartridges!

Sweet Charity, 1969

SOPHIA LOREN · PAUL NEWMA
DAVID NIVEN go from Pleasure Pala

3 great
stars get
together
...and
make
really big
things
happen to
comedy!

Lady L, 1966

Columbia, 1967

▶ *The Birds, 1963*

NOTHING YOU HAVE EVER WITNESSED BEFORE HAS PREPARED YOU FOR SUCH SHEER STABBING SHOCK!

ALFRED HITCHCOCK'S "The Birds"

TECHNICOLOR

"It could be the most terrifying motion picture I have ever made!"
—ALFRED HITCHCOCK

starring
ROD TAYLOR · JESSICA TANDY
SUZANNE PLESHETTE

and introducing
'TIPPI' HEDREN
a fascinating new personality

Screenplay by EVAN HUNTER · Directed by ALFRED HITCHCOCK · A Universal Release

Based on Daphne Du Maurier's classic suspense story!

SOON AT MOTION PICTURE THEATRES ACROSS THE NATIO

THE LAST WAR

A most spectacular film depicting the horrors of a nuclear war that may befall us at any moment.

"THE LAST WAR"

A statement by M. Shimizu,
President, Toho Co., Ltd. Tokyo

The time has come for us to make this picture . . .

Newspapers, radio commentators, scholars, common men — all speak of a dread hovering ominously over the entire world every second of every day. If — we repeat — if this dread should descend upon us, it will result in the destruction of mankind and, perhaps, life itself.

Men of intelligence are taking great pains to avert it. This is indeed commendable; there can never be too much effort exercised toward this end. But still we live in fear that a great war, the Last War may come.

We the Japanese are in a better position than people of any other nation to make a film such as this. We side with no one; we are inimical to no one. "The Last War" is presented as our appeal to the world.

We of the Toho Company are employing every vestige of our technical skill to represent as realistically and appealingly as possible exactly what will happen if this colossal horror befalls us.

It is our sincere hope that by producing and exhibiting this film we can serve the cause of peace.

 TOHO COMPANY, LIMITED   14, 1-CHOME, YURAKU-CHO CHIYODA-KU, TOKYO, JAPAN

Speedway, 1968 ◄ *The Last War, 1961*

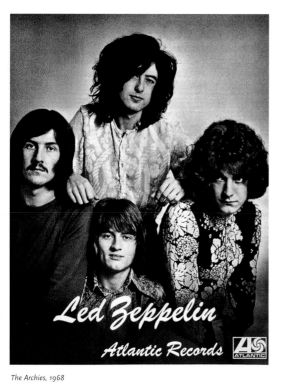

The Archies, 1968

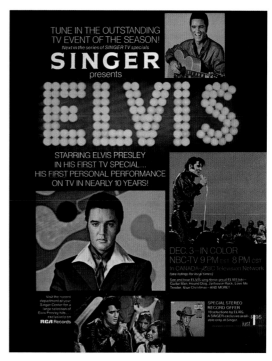

Singer, 1968

Columbia Record Club, 1961

Fashion
& Beauty
200

h.i.s stripe types

(Which type are you?)

Boat Neck. You're modest about your muscles so you cover most of them.

Tank Top. You're proud of your muscles so you show 'em.

Muscle Shirt. You think you have muscles

Crew Neck. You just like stripes.

V-Neck. You think plunging necklines look good on you as well as on the birds.

Stripe of a different type. This one you don't wear. You watch. And she'll return the glances, whichever model you wear. They're cotton knits, each in 8 colors. $4 and $5. h.i.s, 16 E. 34th St., N.Y. 10016

Dan River, 1962 ◄ *H.I.S., 1967*

► *Wrangler, 1964* ►► *Puritan, 1965*

Love him with
Puritan Ban-Lon® Brookviews
of DuPont Nylon

Textralized yarn, 100% Du Pont nylon

**Give him America's favorite knit shirts. Full-Fashioned.
Automatic wash and dry. In 25 amorous colors. $8.95 each.**

PURITAN®

THE PURITAN SPORTSWEAR CORP., 135 W. 50TH ST., NYC

Where to buy it? See last page.

Do the skate:

Skate right, clap hands.

Skate left.

Shake shoulders, roll hands.

Skaters position, lean forward.

Skate forward right, then left.

Cut loose in Career Club™ Shirts

Career Club tapered shirts in cotton broadcloth with new hi-boy roll collar. 15 hot and sweet colors. $4. Slightly higher in the West. Get free dance booklet at your Career Club dealer. Or write to Dance, Truval Shirt Co. Inc., 350 Fifth Ave., N.Y.

ARE YOU READY FOR CENTAUR ?

it's the Massage Cologne ...half man, half beast, all male!

Out of the Wild and Violent days of ancient Greece comes the exciting concept of a Massage Cologne...it's name is **CENTAUR**®

Each morning...each evening massage **CENTAUR** into your torso.

Massage **CENTAUR** into your arms, legs, and loins.

CENTAUR has *no alcohol* to irritate, so it massages with comfort into sensitive areas.

CENTAUR adds a delightful new dimension to your body, a low level aroma that hovers close to the skin for hours, transmits its virile message only in moments of close and intimate contact.

CENTAUR makes no coy promises...finding HER is up to you...then **CENTAUR** gives her the message. She won't say, "What are you wearing?" She will say, *"You smell good!"*

© 1967 Century Creations, Inc., P. O. Box 1499, Santa Monica, Calif.

Introductory
Collectors CLASSIC — 8 oz............ **$10.00**
(Rugged unglazed porcelain, 24K gold finish)
REFILL SET—8 oz. & dispenser pump **$6.50**
TRIAL SIZE — ½ oz.................. **$1.00**

Career Club Shirts, 1967 ◄ *Centaur, 1967*

Groshire/Austin Leeds, 1965 ►

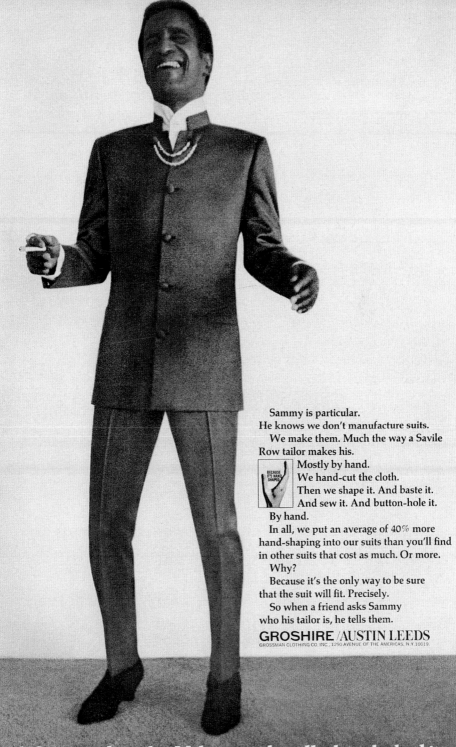

Sammy is particular.
He knows we don't manufacture suits.
   We make them. Much the way a Savile
Row tailor makes his.
          Mostly by hand.
          We hand-cut the cloth.
          Then we shape it. And baste it.
          And sew it. And button-hole it.
By hand.
   In all, we put an average of 40% more
hand-shaping into our suits than you'll find
in other suits that cost as much. Or more.
   Why?
   Because it's the only way to be sure
that the suit will fit. Precisely.
   So when a friend asks Sammy
who his tailor is, he tells them.

GROSHIRE/**AUSTIN LEEDS**
GROSSMAN CLOTHING CO. INC., 1290 AVENUE OF THE AMERICAS, N.Y. 10019.

When they ask Sammy about his Nehru suit, he tells them he had it made.
And he's not putting them on.

Right on Target for Comfort and Smart Styling...

"Deerslayers"

Soft Glove Leather, Traction Crepe Sole and Deep, Full-Length Cushion Insole combine to make Jarman "Deerslayers" the easiest-wearing of all casual shoes. (And the smartest-looking, too!)

Golf shoe, J4627.....................About $17.00
Top: J2127 (also in other colors)....About $13.00
Middle: J2020 (also in other colors).About $13.00
Bottom: J4426 ....About $15.00
(Prices slightly higher in the West)

These shoes

Fit with More Comfor

because every Jarman style is "wear-tested"

The pair of Jarmans you try on has not been worn, of course. But the original model of *every Jarman style* is "wear-tested"—worn under ordinary day-to-day conditions, altered and adjusted until it finally comes up to Jarman's strict standards, and *only* then approved for production. As a result, the finished product has a wonderful "friendliness of fit" you just can't get in other shoes. See your Jarman dealer for a wide selection of "wear-tested" shoes for every occasion.

Available at Jarman dealers and Jarman stores throughout the country. Also Jarman Jrs. for boys.

Jarman, 1965

▶ *Etonic, 1*

Here's TOP QUALITY and AUTHENTIC STYLE

"FAWN"
4" brim; Herringbone Weave; Fawn Color......$5.00

GRAND ENTRY® WESTERN *Straws*

"DESERT SAND"
3½" brim; Pearly Finish; Desert Sand Color......$5.00

SEE THESE SMART STYLES AT YOUR FAVORITE STORE NOW

Make a "grand entry" every time with one of these handsome, authentic western straws. Both feature leather ventilated sweatband with moisture-resistant liner, ventilated crown and enclosed brim wire for easy, permanent shaping. They're soil-resistant, too.

You'll be proud of the good looks and pleased with the top quality workmanship of either style.

If not available, write your nearest distributor for the name of the dealer who handles this quality line of GRAND ENTRY HATS.

GRAND ENTRY HAT CO. • 2625 Sidney Street • St. Louis 4, Mo.

Gillette has a starter kit
for men just starting to shave.

For 99¢, Gillette gives you everything you need to start:
a Super Speed Razor, Super Stainless blades and a two-week supply
of Foamy Shave Cream. Just add water and shave.

Choose the gift
that comes through
with flying colors...

Old Spice

for Dad

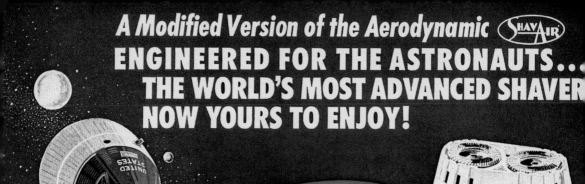

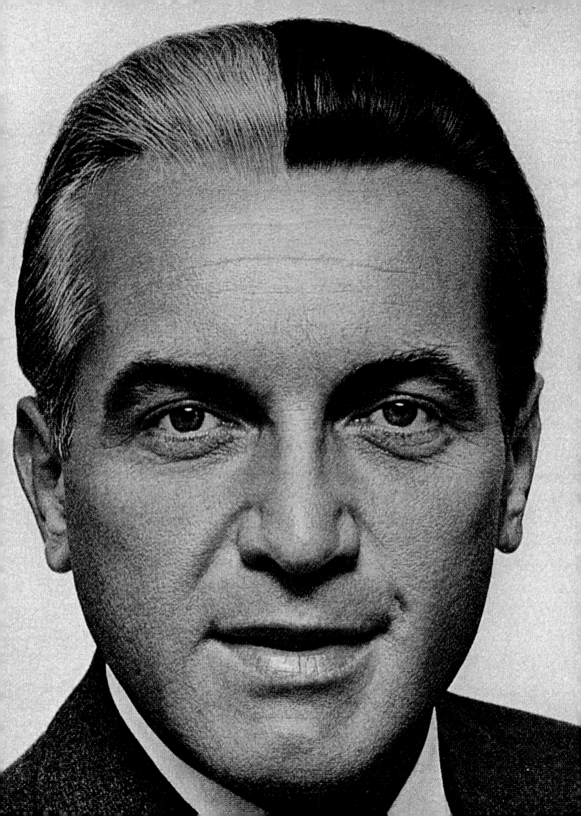

polka dots' place is not on your face

Gloves, gowns—even galoshes—are perfect in polka dots. But complexions—uh-uh. Now, Tussy Medicare has the problem skin well in hand. It hides and helps heal blackheads, pimples—even acne—quickly, comfortably . . . gives your skin a clear lovely look in just three simple steps.

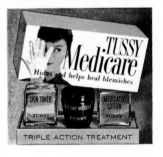

1 To deep-cleanse skin, to remove pore-clogging oil and infection-causing bacteria, and keep them away —Tussy Medicated Creamy Masque. Smoothing, soothing!

2 To stimulate circulation locally, to help float away impurities—Tussy Medicated Skin Toner. Wonderfully cool and refreshing!

3 To make blemishes vanish from view—Tussy Medicated Lotion. Helps dry up excess oil, soften a coarsened skin. A true face saver!

Tussy Medicare Triple-Action Treatment, **$2.95**
Tussy Medicare items, each **$1**
Tussy Medicated Touch-Up Stick for quick cover-ups, **$1**
all prices plus tax

© 1960 TUSSY, 415 PARK AVENUE, NEW YORK

TUSSY *cares for you*

Revlon invents action-now skincare

Un-nouncing 'Un-Lipstick' by Natural Wonder!

'Un-Lipstick'? It's pale, but the shine won't fail. Bare, but the color's there (and never, never changes on your lips). In gleamy little mouthcolors like Ivory Blizzard and Frozen Peaches, Sheer Shiver Pink and Nothing Frosted. 24 shades in all, including the palest frosteds ever put on ice. 'Un-Lipstick'. The liveliest thing that will happen to your lips until you next get kissed.

Natural Wonder 'Un-Lipstick' by REVLON

Cutex, 1961 ◄ *Revlon, 1969*   ► *Max Factor, 1967*   ►► *Charles of the Ritz, 1962*   ►►► *Max Factor, 19*

Cut up, cut out, cut loose with Max Factor's
CALIFORNIA
PINK·A·PADES

**Two pink escapades for lips and fingertips.
Two sheer...two shimmering...too tempting!**

It's the great new color adventure for summer.
Say it Pink-A-Pale (soft, feminine, fragile)
or Pink-A-Fling (lively, zingy, daring).
Wear it either super-sheer or super-frosted.
Any way you play it, have a wild
pink Pink-A-Pade!

California Pink-A-Pades by Max Factor

it's the fashion to wear made-to-order face powder *Charles of the Ritz*

If you're looking for the most luxurious cover-up in the world... don't settle for mink.

Get Pan-Stik® Make-up only by Max Factor.

With Pan-Stik cream make-up your complexion becomes flawless...quietly elegant. Pan-Stik slips on softly. It covers flaws, covers freckles, covers everything but the beauty of you. It hovers softly on your skin, richer than milk, sweeter than honey to the eye (delicately smooth to the touch). No wonder Pan-Stik is known in certain circles as the make-up that great beauties are made of.

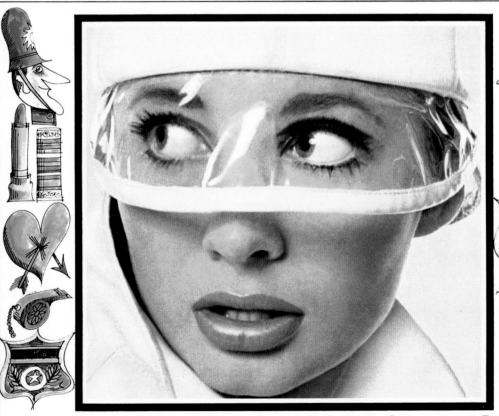

Mitsouko by Guerlain

GENERAL ELECTRIC HAS IT!

General Electric Cares

Bouffant bonnet has reach-in top—for checking dryness.

Air is instantly heated here for faster drying.

Portable...adjustable waist or shoulder strap.

Attractive embossed carrying and storage case.

NEW! FANFARE CLOCK with Mel-O-Tone® alarm to wake you with musical tones. Lighted dial for nighttime. Attractive sandalwood-color case. 3¼ in. high; 5½ in. wide.

TOASTS—AND BAKES! General Electric's Toast-R-Oven* toasts both sides at once. Top-browns...bakes potatoes, frozen foods, and pies...reheats foods, too!
*TM General Electric Company

GENERAL ELECTRIC HAS the Spray, Steam and Dry Travel Iron for touch-up ironing at school and to take on trips. Adapter plugs for foreign travel. Fold-down handle.

General Electric has the hair dryer with an "Instant Heat" unit. It's next to the bonnet for faster hair drying. Large Sally Victor bouffant bonnet...reach-in top to let you check drying. Portable ...lightweight...4 heat selections. Luxurious carrying case, too!

General Electric Company, Housewares Division, Bridgeport, Conn. 06602

Progress Is Our Most Important Product

GENERAL ⒼⒺ ELECTRIC

Yardley of London, 1966 ◄◄   *Mitsouko, 1967* ◄   *General Electric, 1966*   ► *Avon, 1969* ►► *Neutrogena, 1968*

WASH WITH PURE SUNSHINE

NEUTROGENA

HOW TO TEND A GROWING SKIN: WATER IT DAILY WITH THE SUNSHINE SOAP. NEUTROGENA

It puts your sensitive complexion back on the sunny side of Nature, even when kill-or-cure methods have failed you. For this clear amber bar is about as natural as a hunk of pure sunshine. Soothing to upset skin. Mild when it cleans, so your skin doesn't get clobbered in the process. Even more important, Neutrogena® won't leave a sticky soap residue on your face to cause more potential problems, to strip and irritate a troubled skin. In actual tests, it was the only soap that rinsed off completely. The Neutrogena difference is laboratory-proved and patented. And worth trying for yourself, if you'd like Nature back on your side and your skin feeling sunny again. Neutrogena costs $1 at drug and department stores. **Or let us send you a trial-size slice of the sunshine soap plus a FREE 1968 "Sunshine Year" poster-calendar to hang on your wall.** Send just 10c to cover postage and handling to Neutrogena Corporation, Dept. S-1, Box 1660, Santa Monica, California 90406.

is there a female nfl fan
so unfeminine that
she doesn't deserve to
do her own thing?
no,
no.

NFL, 1969

▶ Lektro Set, 1969   ▶ ▶ Kanekalon, 1969

THE 10-MINUTE
(between shampoo)
SET

lektro set.™
and the heat from your dryer
turn on a new set between shampoos.

Just a day or two since you shampooed, and your hair is a put-down. Limp. Lifeless. Straggly. Now, just ten minutes under a dryer can turn on a fresh, bouncy set! New Lektro Set, the ten-minute heat setting spray, turns on a holding set between shampoos! Set your dry hair strand by strand with Lektro Set. In just ten-minutes, the heat from your dryer turns on the special "between shampoos" holding ingredients in Lektro Set. You'll brush out the softest, holdingest set you ever got from dry hair! Try new Lektro Set, by Toni. It can change a put-down to a turn-on in just ten minutes!

Your dryer turns it on! Honest!

Lektro Set by Toni THE 10-MINUTE

Kanekalon's miracle wigs, falls, wiglets, curls take the care out of hair . . . let you pick up and go-go at a minute's notice. No upkeep. No setting. Wash them out in a second, give them a whisk with a comb, and they're ready for anything. Even wind and rain. Wear them now, or stuff them in your handbag for later.

They're made of Kanekalon modacrylic fibers—so natural, so lustrous, so for-real they even fool experts. Match or mix every popular shade, even those want Frosts. Available at fine stores everywh Just be sure you find Kanekalon on the label.

You might be tickled
to know that Lustre-C
is safe for colo
treated hair.

PINK IS FOR GIRLS

That's why girls like Lustre-Creme. It's the only pink shampoo.

Pink says we're rich, so rich your whole head becomes
one great swirl of whipped-cream lather.

Pink says we leave hair soft, and inviting to touch.

And should a certain someone get too close, he'll notice
that we have a delightful "pink" fragrance, too.

Pink, creamy Lustre-Creme. It's the one shampoo
made just for girls. Because pink is just for girls.

You're a girl, aren't you?

Lustre
Creme.

LOTION
SHAMPOO

PINK
IS FOR GIRLS

That's why Lustre-Creme is pink. Because it's made just
for girls. If you don't believe it, just breathe in
Lustre-Creme's pink fragrance. See. It's a little
too delicate for anyone *but* a girl! Now shampoo
with pink Lustre-Creme and feel how truly soft your hair
can be. So soft, it says "touch me." And he will!

Fresh Start, 1966 ◄◄   *Lustre Creme, 1968* ◄   *Lustre Creme, 1969*

Blonding simplified.

© 1966 CLAIROL INC.

Clairol announces new Born Blonde® Lightener in its own complete kit. Lifts out dark color faster than anything even Clairol has ever made!

Now blonding is this simple: (1) Lift the dark color out of your hair with new, speeded-up Born Blonde Lightener, in its own we've-thought-of-everything kit.

(2) Shampoo in one of the 12 pale, shimmery shades of Born Blonde, the no-peroxide toner that took the tears out of blonding. *Who but Clairol could have done it?*

Clairol, 1969

▶ *Clairol, 1969*

It's not always easy to be a woman. But Pursettes® is trying to help. First we created a more absorbent tampon and the only one with a prelubricated tip. So easy to use. It doesn't even need a bulky applicator. And now we've created a tiny fashionable compact to carry your Pursettes. It's made in a variety of swingy, feminine styles and holds four regular Pursettes Tampons or three super-absorbent Pursettes Plus. Such a pretty, simple way to carry your protection. And it's free, with the purchase of any size box of Pursettes.

**Mail to Campana, Dept. LA-96
Batavia, Illinois 60510**

Please send me Tampon Compact(s) marked_____. I am enclosing a box top from Pursettes and 10¢ to cover cost of postage and handling. Check: I am a new Pursettes user ☐; a steady Pursettes user ☐.

Name_____

Address_____

City_____

State_____ Zip_____

Campana reserves right to substitute patterns if necessary. Offer limited to U.S.A. only. Void where taxed, restricted or prohibited by law. Expires December 31, 1969. Allow 3 weeks delivery.

It's nicer than ever
to be a woman.
Stylish Tampon Compacts
by Pursettes.

Pursettes, 1969

▶ *Formfit Rogers, 1969* ▶▶ *Plaza 8, 1966*

Be Some Body.

Start right now with The Stocking Girdle™ which gives you girdle control with pantyhose freedom. Nylon and Lycra® spandex top, stretch nylon legs. In champagne, sun mist, mink mist, silver mist. Petite, medium, long, extra long. $3 in the foundation department of your favorite store.

A DIVISION OF GENESCO, INC. ®REG. TM DUPONT

Formfit Rogers

Sears has gone wild!

The Adventuress set: Go lean. Go lacy. Go live with color. Go wild! With Sears Adventuress Set.

The bra: lace cups on a stretch frame, stretch straps, scoop back. Natural cup with Cordtex® lift. Or contour cup with Wonder-Fil. Both styles under $6. (D cup higher)

The girdle: a new kind of power net that stretches to your measure for proportioned fit, all-over comfort. Spot controlling panels front, side and back. Under $12.

Choose the Adventuress Set (and matching lingerie!) in Adventuress Pink, Bravado Blue, or Desert Beige, all with Beige Lace or Snow Leopard White with White Lace. Charge it on Sears Revolving Charge at any of over 2,500 Sears, Roebuck and Co. locations.

Go wild! At Sears.

Sears

I dreamed I was a knockout

in my *maidenform* bra

Arabesque*... *new Maidenform bra*... has bias-cut center-of-attraction for *superb* separation...insert of elastic for *comfort*...floral circular stitching for the most *beautiful* contours. *White in A, B, C cups, just 2.50. Also pre-shaped (light foam lining) 3.50.*

What's black
and white
and red
all over?

Warner's latest...greatest MERRY WIDOW...that's what!

Revel in the lightest, the loveliest, the *first* Merry Widow *ever* fashioned of 'New Dimension' Lycra, the new elastic fiber Warner's and DuPont worked hand in hand to develop . . . lighter and longer lasting than elastic's ever been! And you can zip *this* Merry Widow . . . solo . . . right up its lacy front! With its new "bare look," low-back flattery, it shapes you in a way that's almost wicked, whittles your middle while it gives a lovely lift with softest of nylon lace cups.* But, remember, darling, if it isn't by Warner's,® it just *isn't a* Merry Widow!® At your nicest stores. #1308. White, Black, Red Pepper. $16.50.

New and Young from Warner's

*(ANTRON® NYLON FRONT, ELASTIC OF NYLON, LYCRA® SPANDEX, POLYESTER)

Sears, 1969 ◄◄ *Maidenform, 1961* ◄ *Warner's, 1960*

I dreamed I drove them wild
in my *maidenform* bra

COUNTERPOINT*...new Maidenform bra made with super-strong Spandex—new, non-rubber elastic that weighs almost nothing at all yet lasts (and <u>controls</u> you) far longer than ordinary elastic. Exclusive "butterfly insert" adjusts size and fit of each cup as it uplifts and separates! Cotton or Spandex back. White. From 2.00.

Maidenform, 1961

▶ *Maidenform, 1961*   ▶▶ *Exquisite Form, 1966*

Rudi even does dresses to match

Halter Bra. Wear it as a bare back halter or convert it to a regular bra. $4.
Petticoat. Short for today's short skirts. $4.

Camise. A camisole slip with the look of a little chemise. $7.

Bikini. Tiny bikini pantie to wear under everything. $2.50.

Strapless Band Slip. Yo won't need a bra with th stretch top band slip. $8.

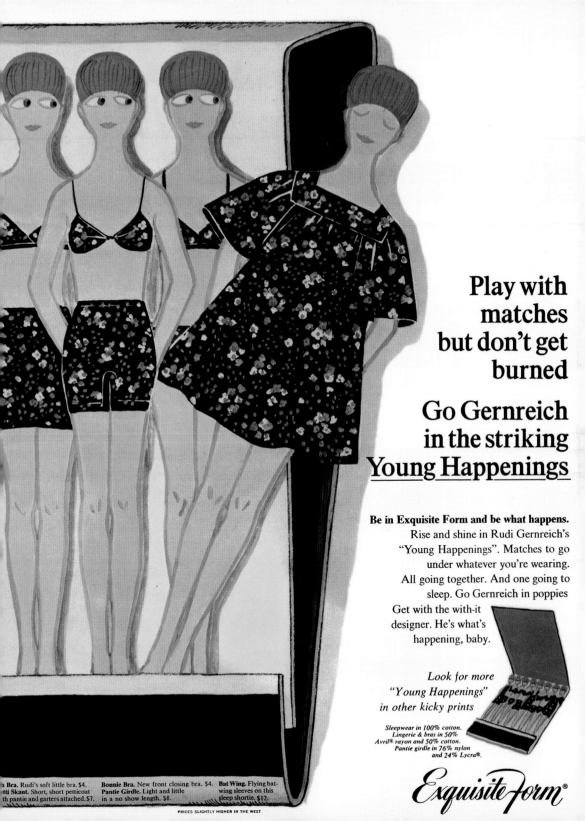

Play with matches but don't get burned

Go Gernreich in the striking <u>Young Happenings</u>

Be in Exquisite Form and be what happens.
Rise and shine in Rudi Gernreich's "Young Happenings". Matches to go under whatever you're wearing. All going together. And one going to sleep. Go Gernreich in poppies Get with the with-it designer. He's what's happening, baby.

Look for more "Young Happenings" in other kicky prints

Sleepwear in 100% cotton.
Lingerie & bras in 50%
Avril® rayon and 50% cotton.
Pantie girdle in 76% nylon
and 24% Lycra®.

h Bra. Rudi's soft little bra. $4.
tti Skant. Short, short petticoat
th pantie and garters attached. $7.

Bonnie Bra. New front closing bra. $4.
Pantie Girdle. Light and little
in a no show length. $8.

Bat Wing. Flying bat-
wing sleeves on this
sleep shortie. $12.

Exquisite Form®

PRICES SLIGHTLY HIGHER IN THE WEST

This is no shape for a girl.

That's why Warner's makes the Concentrate girdle and the Little Fibber bra.

Girls with too much bottom and too little top: Warner's® can reshape you.

We reshape you on the bottom with the Concentrate girdle: Its all-around panels do more for you than a little girdle (they're lined up to help you where you need help most), yet Concentrate doesn't squash you like a heavy girdle.

We reshape your top with the Little Fibber bra. The super-soft fiberfill lining doesn't make a big production out of you. It rounds out your bosom just enough to go with your trimmed-down hips.

All of a sudden, you've got a proportioned body, and your clothes fit better. Warner's calls this a Body-Do.™ You can get fitted for one in any good store.

A BODY-DO FOR THE AVERAGE PEAR: THE LITTLE FIBBER™ CONTOUR BRA, $3. THE CONCENTRATE™ GIRDLE, $12. WARNER SLIMWEAR-LINGERIE. A DIVISION OF THE WARNER BROTHERS COMPANY.

Warner's, 1967

► *Movie Star, 1969*   ►► *Hush Puppies, 1962*

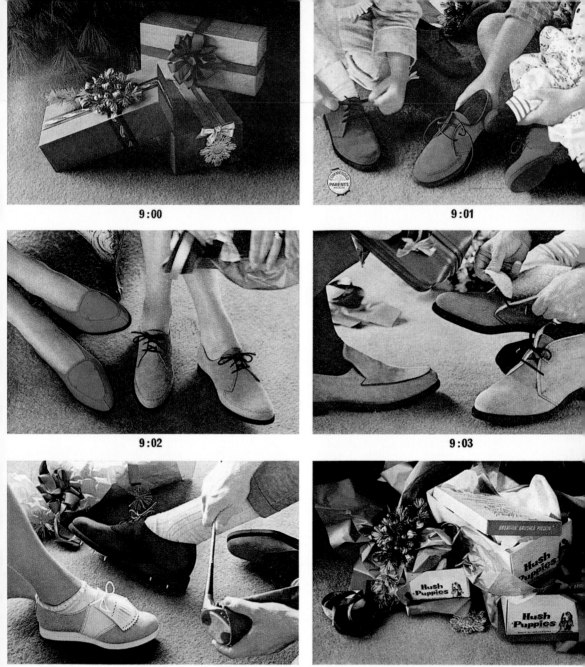

9:00

9:01

9:02

9:03

9:04

(...and a Merry Christmas to all!)

Hush Puppies casuals are always first out of their Christmas wraps. Here's why: 9:01 **EASY-TO-CLEAN** Hush Puppies like these youths' oxfords and girls' oxfords stay clean with an occasional brushing. 9:02 **COLORFUL** women's slip-ons and women's oxfords are two of more than 100 Hush Puppies styles and colors. 9:03 **LIGHTWEIGHT** Hush Puppies, including these men's fleece-lined chukka boots and men's overlay moccasins, weigh less than 12 oz. per shoe. 9:04 **WATER-SHAKING** Hush Puppies, specially tanned to resist water, dirt and soil, include these men's saddle golf shoes and women's saddle golf shoes (with optional kiltie).

Hush Puppie

BREATHIN' BRUSHED PIG
CASUAL SHOES BY WOLV

fun favorite of the family
converse
playtime footwear

Join the lightfooted league! Here's cool, colorful comfort and easy washability, plus the same action-engineered construction, the same quality craftsmanship that have made Converse first in sports footwear for over fifty years. Your champions deserve Converse too!

All-purpose men's-boys' action favorites

Casuals for men and boys in new smart styles

Classic ladies' oxford in style-right fabrics

Child's soft-stepping oxford with protective toe cap

merican made to highest quality standards

VERSE RUBBER COMPANY/ South San Francisco, California

JUST FOR KICKS

ORLON ®

Legs, that's where the action is in Orlon* acrylic. And it all starts where a
short skirt stops. Take your pick of the fun going on, this fall—patterns, tex-
tures, colors. All yum, all swinging in "Orlon". Try them. Just for kicks!

*DU PONT'S REGISTERED TRADEMARK. DU PONT MAKES FIBERS, NOT THE FASHIONS OR STOCKINGS SHOWN.

DUPONT

Better Things for Better Living . . . *through Chemistry*

Take a stand on platforms!

We did!

Give our new platforms a try.
They're fashion's exciting new High-Rise.
Designed to give your look a new
lift. A bolder stance. A broader heel.
Greater footing—with lots of sole.
Escape the last-year look. Come see our collection
of all-new, all-now platforms. At most Sears,
Roebuck and Co. stores.

The Shoe Place at

Sears

the fashion stop

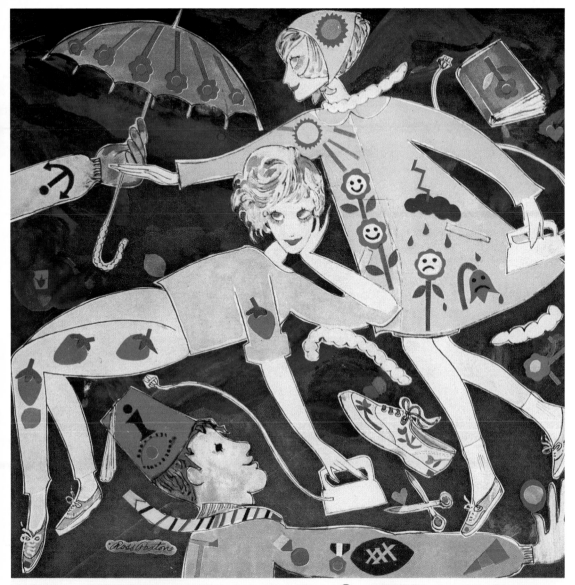

ONE NEIGHBORHOOD BUZZ & HOW IT TURNED INTO A BEE, a beautiful bee with BONDEX
HOT IRON FABRICS

Buzz a friend. Or two. Or three. And have a bee: a beautiful bee with BONDEX—the fantastic fabric that sticks better than a girl's best friend. Here's all you do. Think up a mad and merry motif. And cut it out. Cut it right out of Bondex. Then, hot up your iron. And iron your master-piece in place. Make a Keds® sneaker chic-er. A sweater better. Cop a couple of pretties from this page. Or dig deep for something all your own. Something washing can't woo away. Bondex goes on to stay. (Yes, it's the very same Bondex that's your friend when you mend.) Pray, get some today. Where? At the nearest notions counter.

Bondex, 1961 ◀   *Bondex, 1961*

Suit by Dalton of America

Marked for greatness
This superb suit with the mark of the world's best…pure wool

Excellence. In design, detail, tailoring. That's what you get when a designer *cares*. In fabric, you get the world's best. Pure wool. Wool that drapes gracefully, tailors beautifully. Wool with the natural resilience to keep in shape. Designers of distinction choose wool. They're proud to wear the mark, created

by the Wool Bureau, given only to fashions made of the worl best pure wool. Look for the wool mark. Wherever you fin you find devotion to excellence. Dalton selected pure woo an exciting crochet knit to bring you this dazzling 3-piece The Wool Bureau, Inc., 360 Lexington Ave., New York 17, N

This mark was created by the Wool Bureau, Inc.
It is awarded to quality products made of the world's best pure wool.

Dacron.
It ought to be
a law.

JUNIOR ACCENT thinks 'twould be a crime for pure pizzaz not to have the lasting shape of "Dacron". Thus, this sonic knit that has—a print so bold you can almost hear it. And a fresh so great it goes on forever. And why? Because it's

<u>100% Dacron* polyester.</u> In red/white/navy, yellow/white/black. Sizes 6-16. About $46. Available at Franklin Simon, New York and branches; Town and Country, Des Moines; Joseph Horne Co., Pittsburgh; Frederick & Nelson, Seattle.

*DU PONT'S REGISTERED TRADEMARK. DU PONT MAKES FIBERS, NOT FABRICS OR FASHIONS. EARRINGS BY HATTIE CARNEGIE.

Better Things for Better Living ... *through Chemistry*

Wool, 1964 ◄ *DuPont, 1961*

THE MADNESS OF COTTON

as expressed by Adele Simpson

Great, colorful flowers that explode like fireworks
in a white, white firmament. Cotton made it happen. Cotton
made it the high fashion it is. Wear it and
listen for the murmurs of admiration, the sighs of envy.
National Cotton Council, Box 12285,
Memphis, Tenn. 38112.

COMFORTABLE · CAREFREE
COTTON

Cotton, 1967

▶ *Bill Blass, 1966*

How come all non-conformists look alike?

Maybe it's because the people who select the fashions you'll be wearing think all people who want to be different are the same.

We know better. So we offer you an opportunity to select what you want, not what someone else thinks you want.

And chances are what you select will be different, because it can't be bought in the stores. It can only be sewn.

Every month Simplicity puts out a catalog. The big Simplicity Catalog. It's full of new and newer-than-new fashions.

And if you like, you can make something no one can ever have, except you. Because you choose the patterns and colors and fabrics and trimming. As far-in or as far-out as you like.

We'll be as different as you make us. Which is what makes us different from everyone else.

Simplicity
Sew your own thing

Simplicity, 1969 ◄ *Penney's Rainbow Lane, 1967*

JUST OFF THE PRESS!

The newsy gown they said was too wild to print

The Great
Paper Dress

An Exclusive Holiday Offer from Johnston's Pies
APPLE — PUMPKIN — MINCE

1 25
PLUS 25¢ HANDLING

(AND THAT'S NOT PIE IN THE SKY)

It's so beautiful. Fashion's just-for-fun dress designed by the Scott Paper Company to wrap you in colors so rich and hot (thank heavens the dress is fire-resistant). It's so beautiful. Tie shoulders for easy step-in styling. Side slits to let you kick up a sensation. Wear it at home. Wear it at parties. Wear it without a care because when you're through you just give it the air. It's so beautiful. And it must be yours.

Just look for Johnston's frozen holiday pies: Apple, Pumpkin and Mince with the Paper Dress Offer right on the package. And tucked inside is your order blank. And would you believe that that's not all? With every dress you order, you receive 52¢ worth of Scott Paper product coupons. This is all just so beautiful. And near as your nearest market.

Offer expires January 31, 1967. Void where prohibited, taxed or restricted.

Shy violets not shy enough to seek cover

pop up in a Jantzen Bashful Bikini.

Who wouldn't smile upon nature at its best?

Even more glamorous when wet 15.95.
T.M.

just wear a smile and a Jantzen

Jantzen Inc., Portland 8, Oregon

you're all wet...

but your hairdo isn't!

You're the belle of the beach! Sava-Wave inner rim in Kleinert's fashion s
caps "seals out" water, keeps your hair dry and beautiful. Ondine (sh
hugs head in a cascade of face-flattering petals. New ombré color e
in pink, green, blue, gold, black and orange.
Price $6. Other Sava-Wave caps from $1.25.
Who would have thought of it but Kleinert's.
485 FIFTH AVE., N.Y., N.Y. · TORONTO, CANADA · LONDON, ENGLAND

Kleinert's
SWIM CAPS

Because the sun doesn't stand still...
you need the <u>total</u> <u>eye</u> <u>protection</u> of the ff77˚ Lens

Unless you're wearing Foster Grant sunglasses — you may be getting only partial eye protection.

Because only Foster Grant has the ff77 Lens — the first sunglass lens electronically controlled to protect you at *any* hour, at *any* angle, at *any* season in the sun.

No matter how strong the glare,

the ff77 Lens filters out 77% of the sun's rays — proved by scientific study as the ideal average percentage of filtration.

And unlike polarizing lenses, which admit varying amounts of glare at different angles, the ff77 is uniformly *glare-proof*. You see better — and you *look* better, too.

Your eyes stay clear and bright, free of squint lines — always attractive no matter how strong the glare.

Get *total* eye protection. Get Foster Grant Sunglasses — the *only* sunglasses with the ff77 Lens. From $1 to $5.

*Trademarks of
FOSTER GRANT CO., INC., LEOMINSTER, MASS.

Custom fit frames of *Miracle Nylon* — a revelation in lightweight, comfortable fit.

ONLY **FOSTER GRANT** SUNGLASSES AND **OPTI-CLIPOVERS** HAVE THE

"Fastest tan under the sun-"

"—with maximum sunburn protection!"

say

Paula Prentiss

and

Jim Hutton

Nothing flatters you like a beautiful tan. And . . . Hollywood stars know there's no tan like a Coppertone *suntan*. Millions of sun worshipers agree. That's why Coppertone is America's favorite suntan product . . . *outsells all other brands by far!*

Tests under the Florida sun proved why. Conducted by eminent skin specialists, they showed that with Coppertone's "sun-balanced" formula you get the fastest tan possible with maximum sunburn protection . . . *a marvelously deep, rich, natural tan!*

There's no skin-drying alcohol in Coppertone—no worry about ugly dryness or peeling. Coppertone is *good* for your skin! Its rich lanolin and other emollients keep skin soft, smooth.

So, get the *best* tan under the sun—get Coppertone. Nothing else will do!

Paula and Jim star in "THE HORIZONTAL LIEUTENANT" *an MGM release*

COPPERTONE *Suntan Lotion* NON-OILY. PROMOTES FAST TAN. PROTECTS AGAINST SUNBURN. CONDITIONS SKIN.

COPPERTONE ®

AMERICA'S NO. 1 LINE OF SUNTAN PRODUCTS

The only really complete line—with a product for every need:

Don't be a paleface

LOTION: the popular favorite for "balanced" tanning and sunburn protection.
OIL: for those who want deepest tan and require less protection.
CREAM: for maximum "stay-on" during swimming or long exposure.

SPRAY: in handy aerosol can—for convenience, and speedy application to all parts of the body.
NOSKOTE: gives special protection to nose and extra exposed spots.
LIPKOTE: soothing to sore lips!

Save—always ask for the largest size

Coppertone is a registered trademark of Plough, Inc.

Also available in Canada

Children, blondes, redheads, all sensitive skins need COPPERTONE SHADE

Is your skin especially sensitive? Do you burn easily? Then ask for Coppertone SHADE. Contains extra amounts of Coppertone's famous sunscreen ingredient to give you extra sunburn protection while you get a beautiful tan.

Coppertone, 1962

I dreamed I was

HAT BY JOHN FREDERICS

WANTED
in my Maidenform* bra

'FRAME-UP'* new bra with 3-way support

Embroidered panels frame, outline and separate the cups. Extra-firm supports at the sides give you extra uplift. Stretch band at the bottom keeps the bra snug and securely in place. It's a 'Frame-up'—in A, B, C cups.

*REG. U. S. PAT. OFF. ©1963 BY MAIDENFORM, INC., MAKERS OF BRAS, GIRDLES, SWIMSUITS

IT'S A STEAL, AT
$1⁵⁹

Maidenform, 1963

Isn't that Raquel Welch
behind those Foster Grants?

(Yes indeed. See her in "Bandolero," from 20th Century Fox.)

To remove any further speculation, we'll own up. That is Miss Welch.

But, as you can see, our Foster Grants (known to many as the Sunglasses of the Stars) have done it again. They've given Raquel a new dimension. Several in fact.

One moment she's capricious. Then contented. Now candid. Even coy.

That, kind heart, is the Spell of the Shades.

Long, long ago folks wore sunglasses only when they were under the sun. Now they wear them from sun up till sun up. From New Year's Day till New Year's Eve.

In every kind of weather. Everywhere.

Sunglasses have become funglasses.

We can't tell you how happy that makes us, since Foster Grant is clearly the leader in the anti-glare business.

We have more styles in more colors than anybody.

And they all have ff77 lenses that meet U.S. Government standards for eye protection (standards a lot of expensive imports don't meet).

Now, if somebody mentioned sunglasses, who would you think of first?

Besides Raquel Welch.

© FOSTER GRANT. LEOMINSTER

"So you admit you didn't come to Zermatt just to climb the Matterhorn."

"Am I doomed, C. B., to play the sex symbol in an age of flower children?"

"... and now, love, you know all my secrets."

"If you really wanted to hang on to Rhodesia, Sir Robert, why didn't you tell me?"

"Any man who straightens his tie as often as you just has to be hiding something."

"Matador, you're looking at a woma who wants more than a moment of tru

"But you've just got to see me, doctor. I woke up in the dead of night feeling practically middle-aged."

"With 5,000 Brahmas up on the mesa and 30 hands down with the mumps, Mary Beth, I reckon I'll just have to pass up the Paris openings this spring."

"We all make mistakes, Mr. Bond. Now buckle up your trench coat and get out of here."

Isn't that Mia Farrow behind those Foster Grants?

MIA FARROW has become a name to conjure with. Our delicate task was to discover whether our Foster Grants could conjure with Mia, could play tricks with her. With a star so young, we couldn't be sure.

We needn't have worried. No sooner had she slipped behind her first pair than the metamorphosis began. You can see for yourself.

That's the fun of sunglasses. We call it the Spell of the Shades.

Nobody's sure why, but that mysterious something that comes over people behind sunglasses is probably the reason so many people are wearing them today. People who've never been near a beach, who never

come out 'til the sun goes down. That's why they've got wardrobes of them, where they used to own just a pair. That's why they're as popular in Hong Kong as they are in Hollywood.

What's more, millions of them are Foster Grants. Because we happen to be #1 in the business. Far and away.

Of course Mia doesn't even care about that. She probably doesn't even care that Foster Grant 877 lenses pass strict U.S. eye protection tests, while many of the fancy-priced imports fail.

Does she care that we make more styles, in more colors, in more sizes than anybody—from $1 to $5? We do, even if she doesn't. So there.

"Frankly, mother, I'd be a lot happier if you didn't even try to Watusi."

"Incomparable I may be, Gregory, but you can't seriously expect me to play a love scene opposite that."

Foster Grants, 1964

WILD, WILD, WILD NEW BEACHGLASSES!

(and they're polarized!)

BOYWATCHERS
One continuous Rigly peek-hole curving behind your eyes. In cheery Pink, Style Orange, Ingenue White, Gold-try Fresh, Plaka Blue.

DAYTONA

THUNDERBIRD

DISCOTHEQUE

MAYCO
california

Foster Grants, 1968 ◄   May Co., 1965

How

to enjoy

the sun

...in style

BAUSCH & LOMB

Ray-Ban

the most distinguished name in sun glasses

Frame your eyes in flattery . . . protect your eyes in bright sunlight with Ray-Ban Sun Glasses. They filter out the harsh glare that makes you squint, that causes fine wrinkles. For the best eye protection . . . the protection ordinary sun glasses cannot give . . . insist on B&L Ray-Ban Sun Glasses with G-15 neutral gray or green lenses of finest optical glass.

11 exciting frame styles, 42 fashionable colors. From $6.50. At optical offices and select stores everywhere. Bausch & Lomb Optical Co., Rochester 2, N. Y.

Wear glasses? Enjoy the comfort of genuine Ray-Ban lenses in your prescription. You can get them in single vision or bifocal types, where you obtained your present glasses.

"Satire", Tan and White   "Myth", Blue Sparkle   "Sun-Gay", Red and White

Model is wearing Ray-Ban "Marcelle", in new Green Shadow

Ray-Ban, 1960

269

Food & Beverage
270

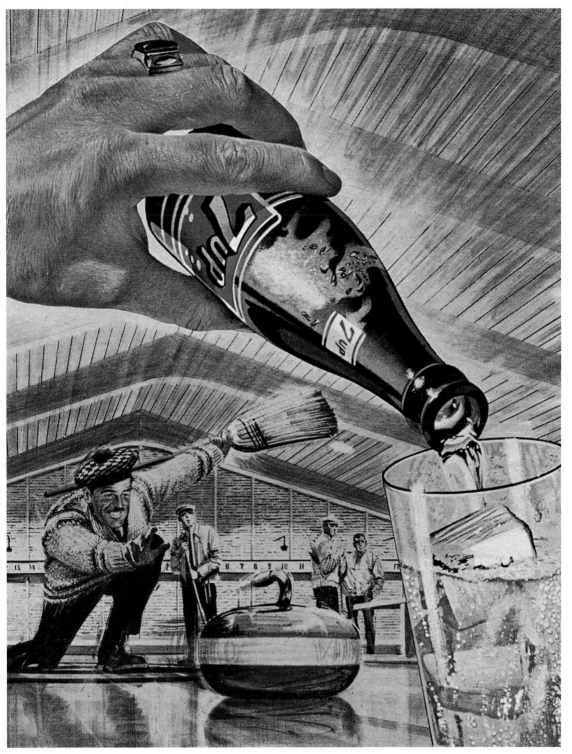

Curtiss Candy, 1962 ◄◄ *Kellogg's, 1962* ◄   *7-Up, 1964* ▶ *7-Up, 1960*

Big HANG-UPS
FROM Wink.

LOVE

SELF PORTRAIT

ADAM COSMO

2000 LIGHT YEARS

WANT A SET OF ORIGINAL PETER MAX POSTERS?
YOU CAN GET THEM ONLY FROM WINK.

If you could buy these colorful 24" x 36" posters in a store, you'd pay $4.00 for the pair, but you can have *two for just $1.25* plus the red stars (or facsimile, or bottle-cap liner) from any Wink carton. Want all four? $2.00 does it. Get a whole new feeling with Wink.

Wink turns on your taste with a pop pop tingle. And these pop pop Peter Max posters turn on any room. Get a couple . . . or get all four. Fill out the coupon below and mail it today. You wouldn't want to be the last one on your block to get these hang-ups, would you?

CANADA DRY MAKES IT.

Dr Pepper, 1960 ◄ *Wink, 1968*

► *Tab Cola, 1966*

The Now Taste of Tab.

Tab. Trimmed down in sweetness, so it's a little bit dry.
With 1 crazy calorie in every 6 ounces.
Like everything now a little bit crazy, but wow.
The now taste of Tab.
That's what's happening. To the nicest shapes around.

TRADE-MARK ®

outflavors

any single juice!

Your happy tastebuds will tell you
a thing or two about V-8. They'll tell
you V-8's *all* flavor—flavor 8 juices
deep! Flavor so fresh it practically
smiles at you. So lively it never ever
bores you at breakfast.

Vital statistics on V-8 Vegetable
Juices: fewer calories than fruit juice...
important vitamins and minerals
...choice of four sizes, from the little
6-ounce individual size to the large
46-ounce size that every V-8 lovin'
family needs.

V-8
Cocktail
VEGETABLE JUICES

V-8 is a trademark of
Campbell Soup Company

V-8 Juice, 1960

▶ *Coca-Cola, 1965* ▶▶ *Nestle's Keen, 1964*

What's
got
into
Tang?

NEW NEW NEW

INSTANT
Tang
BRAND

BREAKFAST
DRINK

More Vitamins C and A

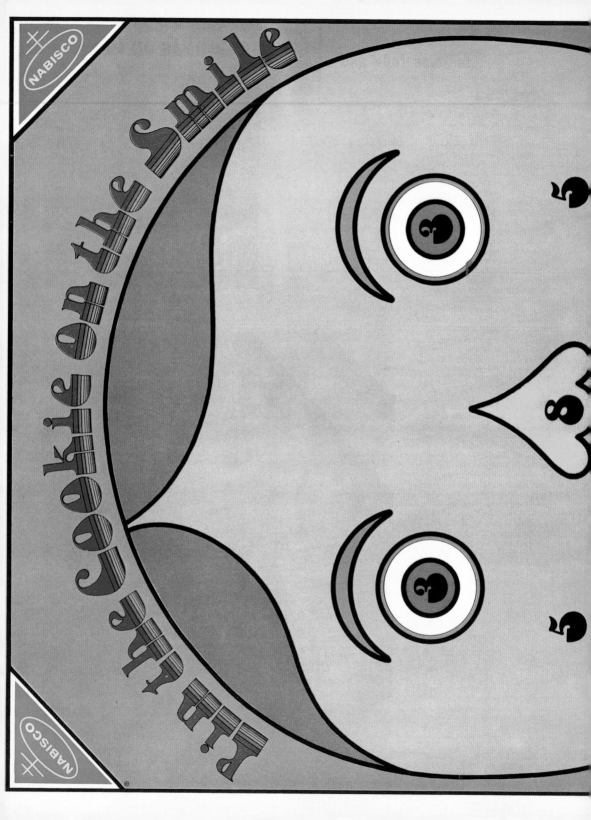

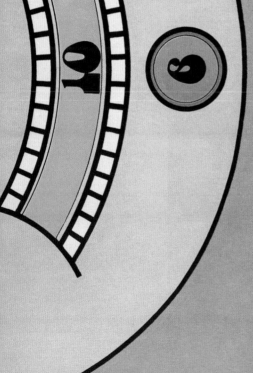

DIRECTIONS FOR PLAYING

Pin the Cookie on the Smile

Place funny face on wall. First "Pinner" step forward and choose your favorite NABISCO cookie from the five cookie cut-outs. Put on blindfold. Turn around three times. Think NABISCO—real hard. Get ready. Aim. Pin! Now check your luck. Hit near a number? Take that many cookies. Missed the funny face altogether? Put one back. Hit the smile? Wowee! Take two of each kind. Now enjoy your NABISCO cookies (all delicious!) while the next "Pinner" tries his luck.

NABISCO Chocolate Chip Cookies. Chocolate-lovers take notice! You never saw so many bits of chocolate in a cookie. Rich, rich morsels lavishly scattered all through the tender, golden brown texture.

FIG NEWTONS Cakes. Fresher, moister, fig jam makes FIG NEWTONS so plump and juicy and chewy. Double-wrapping keeps the jam juicy fresh, the golden cake tender. Only NABISCO makes FIG NEWTONS.

OREO Creme Sandwich. Inside—the richest, creamiest filling ever. Outside — the best, chocolate-y rich wafers made with dutch cocoa and pure chocolate. That's OREO. America's all-time favorite cookie.

LORNA DOONE Shortbread. More butter in the batter gives LORNA DOONE that extra-tender, mouth-melting texture. Rich and good when you eat them just plain, and even better with strawberries and cream.

NABISCO Vanilla Wafers. Eggs make the difference, make NABISCO Vanilla Wafers so much better than ordinary ones. Thinner, richer, crisper, delicately airy-light.

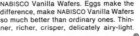

The Wise Old Owl Says:

"Be Queen of the block
and save money too
... treat the kids to

Brach's
Halloween Candies

When youngsters cry "Trick or Treat", they want the best candy. That's why it's smart to serve Brach's! All the magic shapes, exciting flavors and enchanting colors make Brach's *the* Halloween candy tradition. Bewitch them with pure candy and pure fun ... at prices that let you buy plenty. So be a smart shopper and Queen of the block, too ... buy Brach's Halloween candies.

FREE Look for Brach's "Candy Owl" masks on many of the Brach's "Trick or Treat" Candies.

Brach's makes <u>59</u> kinds of Halloween Candies

never saw a pink elephant

until Baker's Coconut

luffy, flavory Baker's Angel Flakes! It's imagination in a box, because it ves you so many fanciful ideas. Like Pink Elephant Cut-Up Cake: Just ake two 9-inch layers. Cut a 1½″ ring from one and then vide the ring for trunk and legs. Put 'em all together and spread with a fluffy pink frosting, then sprinkle with Baker's Angel Flake Coconut. Use a cookie for an ear, a mint and gumdrop for a eye, a licorice twist for a tail. A different wild cake on each package...

BAKER'S
Angel Flake
COCONUT
SWEETENED

*Cut-Up Cake Ideas
Inside Package* ▶

Bake a zoo! For a booklet of animal "Cut-Up Cakes", send 15¢ to Baker's Coconut, "Cut-Up Cakes", Box 750-1, Kankakee, Illinois.

Oh, Mamma Mia!... wait till you taste Meat Balls...made with Hunt's Tomato Paste

Hunt's Hunt's

TOMATO PASTE SALSA DI POMIDORO

the paste with the Sunny Italian Flavor
Hunt...for the best

ITALIAN MEAT BALLS *with Noodles*

"This Italian-style dish, *everyone* enjoys—especially when you use that good Hunt's Tomato Paste. Mamma Mia! It's the way to get the rich, tomato flavor in your Italian-style recipes—just like home! I know your family will like it."

2 eggs, well beaten	1 teasp. salt	1 teasp. dried sweet basil
1 lb. ground beef	3 tablsp. Wesson,	1 teasp. salt; dash pepper
1 clove garlic, minced	pure vegetable oil	½ teasp. sugar
2 tablesp. minced parsley	2 6-oz. cans Hunt's Tomato Paste*	1 lb. noodles or ½ lb.
¼ cup grated Parmesan cheese	3 cans hot water	spaghetti, cooked

Mix together first six ingredients. With wet hands form into about 16 balls (mixture will be quite soft). Brown slowly in hot oil, shaking pan frequently to keep balls round. Blend Hunt's Tomato Paste with remaining ingredients. Pour over meat balls. Cover and simmer 1 hour. Serve over cooked noodles or spaghetti. Makes 4 servings. Hunt Foods, Inc., Fullerton, California

*Hunt's Tomato Paste is pure tomato, concentrated to a thick paste. Use in any recipe for true tomato flavor, a spoonful to a can full, depending on the recipe. Generally, add it to the water or liquid, then to the other ingredients.

Del Monte, 1962 ◄   *Hunt's, 1961*   ► *Nabisco Ritz, 1968*   ► ► *Campbell's Soup, 1965*

MOM ART

ny contemporary collection of the creative masterpieces mother cooks up in the kitchen will no doubt
nclude a can of Campbell's Tomato Soup. That red and white can is a model of practicality. Here's a
ugh outline of the clever things mother can do with it: **1** Serve it hot and buttered in cups or mugs.
Top hamburgers with it. **3** Slice yesterday's roast and reheat the slices in it. **4** Serve it in bowls gar-
ished with parsley or a dollop of sour cream. **5** Paint pork chops delicious with it. **6** Bake fish
llets in Campbell's Tomato Soup. However Mom does it, it's an art. Ask Pop.

They always eat better when you remember the soup

did you ever see a fat Chinese?

This message is brought to you as a public service by the Rice Council of America. Switch from routine to rice!

Campbell's Soup, 1968 ◄   *Rice Council of America, 1967*   ► *Cracker Barrel Cheese, 1960*   ►► *Campbell's Soup, 1968*

NATURALLY FROM **KRAFT**

It's <u>more</u> than good cheese...

It's a real pleasure...

It's Cracker Barrel !

SHARP
Cracker Barrel
Cheese
NATURAL CHEDDAR
from KRAFT

SHARP
Cracker Barrel Cheese
NATURAL CHEDDAR *from* KRAFT

Only the **very finest cheddar** is selected by Kraft's cheese experts to wear the proud name of Cracker Barrel brand. Each cut is **marked for flavor**—Sharp, Extra Sharp, or Mellow. And sealed in foil so you get this superb natural cheese **as fresh as though it had been cut before your very eyes.** It's always great cheddar . . . **(no guessing!)** . . . when the cheese you set out is Cracker Barrel brand in the handy stick or traditional wedge.

HAVE A BOWL!

Campbell's Pop-Art Bowl is yours for 60¢ and a label from each of Campbell's 3 Noo Noodle-O's Soups!

Noo Golden Vegetable Noodle-O's Eleven garden vegetables in a solid gold broth with oodles and boodles of circular noodles!

Tomato-Beef Noodle-O's A noo noodle treat with good ground beef in a sassy tomato soup. And a mob of Noodle-O's!

Chicken Noodle-O's Tender chicken in a bright, full-flavored broth with spoonable unspillable noodles!

The Non-Skid Noodle Soups! M'm! M'm! Neat!

Please send me _____ Pop-Art Bowls. I enclose 60¢ and one label from each of Campbell's three Noodle-O's Soups for each bowl ordered.

POP-ART BOWL: P.O. Box 440, Maple Plain, Minnesota 55359

Name _____

Address _____

City _____ State _____ Zip _____

Offer expires March 31, 1969. Please allow 3 weeks for handling. Offer good only in U.S.A. and Puerto Rico. Void if prohibited by law. Offer may be withdrawn at any time.

Special offer for boys and girls who eat their vegetables

4-foot Jolly Green Giant Rag Doll $3.50

with 2 labels from any Green Giant products

Maybe this is just the fellow you need at your house to help get the children going on their vegetables. He's a soft, cuddly 4-foot version of the Green Giant. And he's stuffed with lightweight styrene fluffing so he won't lose his shape.

Actually, the Green Giant puts up vegetables so good that children go for them as much as grownups. And the two cans you buy to get this doll will be gone before you know it. Order your Green Giant® Rag Doll today. It's an ideal Christmas gift.

GREEN GIANT®

Good things from the garden.

richer in NATURAL corn cream!

Not just good eating ... *superb* eating, that's Libby's Cream Style Corn. It's pedigreed ... bred to produce plump, juicy kernels; then knowingly blended to start the flow of that rich natural corn cream. The flavor, the texture are your tests that Libby's is the superior brand.

Corn and Wiener Roast—In baking dish, stir 2 tbsp. prepared mustard into 2 #303 cans Libby's Cream Style Corn. Add 8 wieners, gashed and stuffed with sharp cheese. Dot corn with butter and bake in mod. oven 20 min. *Libby, McNeill & Libby, Chicago 4, Ill.*

Libby's cream·style corn

Stokely, 1965 ◄◄   *Green Giant, 1962* ◄   *Libby's, 1961*   ► *Kentucky Fried Chicken, 1968*

North America's Hospitality Dish...

COLONEL SANDERS' RECIPE
Kentucky Fried Chicken
"It's finger lickin' good"

YOU'LL LIKE STAR-KIST TUNA TOO

(Just look for the fisherman with the earring)

© 1960, Star-Kist Foods, Inc.

Drink a can of Metrecal®* and you've had the nutrition of steak, potatoes, peas and carrots. But not the calories. Metrecal has only 225.

(And it comes in 14 different flavors—every one right out of an ice cream parlor.)

Metrecal for lunch and some common sense at other meals will help keep your weight right where you want it.

Two Metrecal meals a day (lunch and dinner), and you can lose weight steadily.

As for 3 a day, talk it over with your doctor first. You might disappear.

The Metrecal steak.

About this picture: Our photographer said, "Since Metrecal's a complete meal, let's shoot it like one."

Let Miss Sunbeam help you make

June A MONTH OF *Fun-days!*

Patio Suppers

Family Picnics

A SYMBOL OF MEMBERSHIP IN AND QUALITY CONTROL BY QUALITY BAKERS OF AMERICA COOPERATIVE, INC

© BY Q.B.A. COOP, INC.

IT'S MEALS-ON-WHEELS MONTH: Get out with the family, relax for fun and easy living! Fill your food calendar with picnics, patio suppers, backyard barbecues! And take along the extra energy and nutrition in Sunbeam Bread, fresh as all outdoors! Look for little Miss Sunbeam on every loaf you buy. She's the smiling symbol of America's finest in quality baked foods.

Sunbeam Bread

Quality Guaranteed, Locally Baked, Nationally Advertised.

FRESH AS ALL OUTDOORS!

Furniture
& Appliances
302

Armstrong, 1965 ◄◄   *Monarch, 1964* ◄   *Congoleum-Nairn Flooring, 1960*   ► *Knoll Associates, 1960*

18 disks of foam rubber neatly arranged on steel shafts support you comfortably on this Marshmallow Loveseat by George Nelson.

Herman Miller Furniture Co. Los Angeles, Cal.

You can cram for exams
read in bed
spotlight a painting
make it a night-light
play the piano
type your homework
rock the baby
do your nails
pay your bills
highlight your objets d'art
reread your love letters
sort your sea shells
and do it beautifully, too...with

LYTEGEM

THE NEW HIGH-INTENSITY LAMP

Lytegem's clean, pure design goes
beautifully with any decorating style.
Pivots at the base, swivels at the
head. Telescopes to any position, in
any direction—puts the right amount
of light right where you want it!
(Even wall-mounted.) In a wide
range of decorator colors, with pure
white, efficient lighting equal to
conventional lamps with 100-watt
bulbs, plus an exclusive built-in anti-
glare band. (See Baton, the only two-
light, single-shade, high-intensity
lamp. Perfect for home and office!)
$17.95 INCLUDING EXTRA BULB, AT
FINE STORES EVERYWHERE.

LIGHTOLIER®

SHOWN HERE
ACTUAL SIZE

Herman Miller, 1960 ◄ Lightolier, 1965   ► Goodfoam Chairs, 1961

Kitchen carpets have to be practical.
Masland made them practically elegant.

The typical kitchen carpet would be a lot more at home in an office building.
Or maybe in somebody's garage. Because, frankly, that's what it was made for.
Neither rain nor sleet nor chicken soup could penetrate that formidable surface.
But alas, the typical kitchen carpet has a face that only a carpet salesman could love.

So Masland created the Un-Typical Kitchen Carpet of
DuPont nylon—carpets with enough color and style to stand
up to paisley refrigerators and vinyl-covered walls.

Galore, shown here, is only one of four shags Masland
makes of DuPont filament nylon, certified "501". They're
all wear-resistant and spot resistant. Spills clean up easily.

All four are as practical as a kitchen carpet should be.
And as elegant as a kitchen carpet can be.

This carpet approved for kitchen use by

The Magic of
Masland
Carpets.

C. H. MASLAND & SONS

Finally, paneling designed for a woman.

AVOCADO OAK

Avocado flavors oak with fashion: subtle color—warm wood.

The wood is real, too—with a family-proof finish and it's earned the Good Housekeeping Seal. See new Chateau™ Avocado Oak. One of 25

Chateau panels at your Georgia-Pacific registered building materials dealer. It's the paneling designed for the decorator in you.

GEORGIA-PACIFIC/THE GROWTH COMPANY
Portland, Oregon 97207

Marlite Paneling, 1969 ◀ *Georgia-Pacific, 1968*

Another Frigidaire Space Age Advance

The Gemini 19... NEW REFRIGERATOR-FREEZER TWIN

Space Age fashions from Harper's Bazaar. Dress designs by John Kloss

Model shown FPD-19VK available in white and 4 colors

A complete food storage center...less than a yard wide

← 35¾" →

Not just another refrigerator-freezer, but a storage center for all your fresh and frozen foods. More than 19 cubic feet of storage space. And all in less than 36 inches of kitchen space. Look at the enormous 244-lb. freezer section on the left. It's pure convenience. A freezer you can get to without standing on tiptoe...without bending low. Now take a nice top-to-bottom look at the 12.12 cu. ft. refrigerator section. Big enough for the biggest family of biggest eaters.

Adjustable, removable shelves. Need extra room? Just remove a shelf and place it in another position. You can arrange three shelves in the refrigerator and one in the freezer to suit yourself.

Meat Tender keeps meats fresh up to 7 days. Has its own chilled air supply that keeps meats safely at the edge of freezing.

Ice Ejector. Ends mess of getting out ice. Just set the tray on the Ice Ejector, flip the handle and you have ice cubes instantly, easily. Handy server holds 80 cubes, with another 60 waiting in the trays.

You'll never defrost again—ever. In both the refrigerator and the freezer you can enjoy shelf after shelf of completely usable, easily reachable Frost-Proof space. Frigidaire Advanced Frost-Proof system means frost never forms—not in the refrigerator, not in the freezer.

The Power Capsule—the revolutionary space age successor to the old-fashioned compressor—is at the heart of the Gemini 19. New power for more space and new features. Whisper silent. Made with incredibly wear-resistant materials—the divider block, one of 3 moving parts, is made of a satellite-type material which has a resistance to wear 4 times greater than highest grade steel.

See the amazing Gemini 19. Now on special display at many Frigidaire dealers during **NATIONAL FRIGIDAIRE WEEK**

The Gemini 19

FRIGIDAIRE

Frigidaire, 1966

▶ *Tappan, 1961*

Maverick

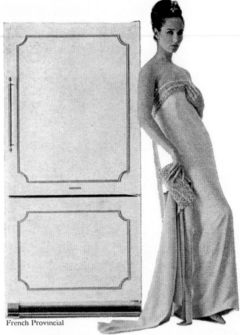

French Provincial

One-Eyed Jack

Scenic

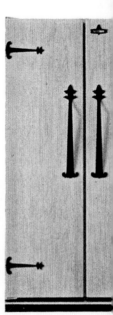

Country Store

Hacienda

Runabout

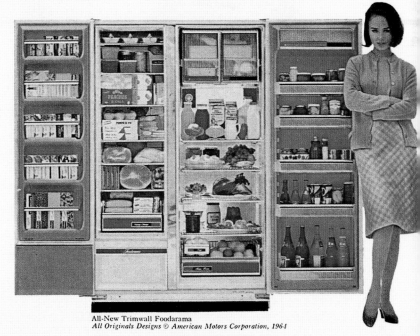

All-New Trimwall Foodarama
All Originals Designs © American Motors Corporation, 1964

Clean without slaving... and feel like a queen!

Backache? Bruised knees?

Try the stand-up way to oven-clean. Model above, RCI-75-60, Double Pull 'N Clean Ovens.

A FRIGIDAIRE *only*
THE PULL'N CLEAN OVEN!

Now yours in either compact 30-inch or full 40-inch 1960 electric ranges

The scour-saving, hour-saving Pull 'N Clean Oven is here in ranges for every budget!

No longer need you stoop, stretch or squat on hands and knees. The whole oven pulls out to clean ... pushes back like a drawer.

Choose from 8 sleek new ranges—with single or double Pull 'N Clean Ovens in 40-inch models; and in 30-inch models with or without French doors; many in 5 Kitchen Rainbow Colors or White.

You'll cook with less work and new joy.

EASIER TO CLEAN—ALL OVER!
EASIER TO COOK—ALL OVER!
Broil without spattering! Famous Radiant Wall Spatter-Free Broiler Grill.
New! Infinite Heat Controls on surface units let you set any cooking heat.
New! Heat-Minder Unit with "degree" settings. Cook on top of the range as accurately as in the oven.
Easy-to-use, easy-cleaning clockwise controls. Lift-Up, Stay-Up Surface Units.

 Product of General Motors

New! French doors on the Pull 'N Clean Oven...open and close at a touch. You can own this magnificent 30-inch Frigidaire Range Model RCI-39-60 for a few dollars a week. See your Frigidaire Dealer.

FRIGIDAIRE ADVANCED APPLIANCES DESIGNED WITH YOU IN MIND

◀ *Kelvinator, 1965 Frigidaire, 1966*

▶ *Whirlpool, 1967*

The refrigerator with a thousand faces.

No matter how beautiful a refrigerator looks when you buy it, after a while it can get terribly boring. But no more.

You can own the new Whirlpool Connoisseur Twin for the next 20 years and change its looks every day without repeating yourself once. Match or contrast your kitchen curtains, walls, cabinets or floor.

How does it work?

The doors have frames around them. To change decor, just insert the material of your choice: curtain fabric, wallpaper, floor vinyl, ¼″ plywood . . . even a photo of your favorite husband. Do you have to be a mechanic? Ma'am you don't even have to be a man. Incidentally, the refrigerator comes in 4 edged colors: sapphire, copper, avocado, and fawn . . . or classic white.

Of course our new refrigerator is more than just a decorator's dream. It's no-frost, with a capacity of over 21 cubic feet, which is the equivalent of a full-size refrigerator *and* a full-size freezer. You can order it with or without an automatic ice-maker. And you yourself can change doors to swing left or right from the sides or the center.

Maybe all this is wasted on you—maybe you don't need a new refrigerator. But, ma'am, don't you wish you did?

Whirlpool CORPORATION

What a wonderful feeling to live with flameless electric comfort conditioning

Turn the page to see 15 special benefits you can enjoy in any home, old or new!

FLAMELESS ELECTRIC CLOTHES DRYING adds so much to the joy of total electric living. All of your clothes come out sunshine fresh. And a modern electric dryer can be put anywhere because no special flue installation is required.

Throughout America, this Gold Medallion identifies modern homes in which families enjoy total electric living with flameless electric home heating and appliances.

YOU LIVE BETTER ELECTRICALLY · Edison Electric Institute, 750 Third Ave., N.Y. 10017

The Temptation of Beautyrest Another story about the kind of comfort

that's kind to your back. The highway man came riding, riding up to the motel door. And when his traffic-tired eyes spotted the "Beautyrest®" sign, he knew that he and his Bess had found the Oasis. Can't you almost hear him saying to her: "Let the unpacking wait, old girl. Drop everything. It's revival time for the road-weary. Your Beautyrest awaits."

Single-bed comfort in a double bed! Because each spring is separate, the heaviest husband cannot disturb his wife's rest. **The best costs the least!** All tests by the United States Testing Co. prove Beautyrest lasts 3 times longer than ordinary mattresses. So Beautyrest, firm or extra firm, at $79.50, is least expensive to own. Another reason why more people, including smart motel hosts, insist on Beautyrest. **Beautyrest by Simmons**

NEW YORK

Herbert Matter

YORK IS KNOLL'S NEW UPHOLSTERY WOOL FOR HOME AND OFFICE, COUCHES AND CHAIRS. A SUBTLE CHANGE IN CLASSIC HOUNDSTOOTH SIMPLIFIES THE WEAVE SO THAT THE PATTERN WORKS IN ANY DIRECTION. THE NEAREST KNOLL SHOWROOM HAS ALL 16 COLORS TO SHOW YOU.

KNOLL ASSOCIATES, INC. 320 PARK AVENUE NEW YORK N.Y. 10022

Showrooms in: Atlanta Boston Chicago Cleveland Dallas Detroit Los Angeles Miami Philadelphia St. Louis San Francisco Seattle Washington, D.C.
International: Argentina Australia Austria Belgium Brazil Canada Finland France Germany India Iran Italy Mexico Netherlands Norway Spain Sweden Switzerland Tunisia Uruguay Venezuela

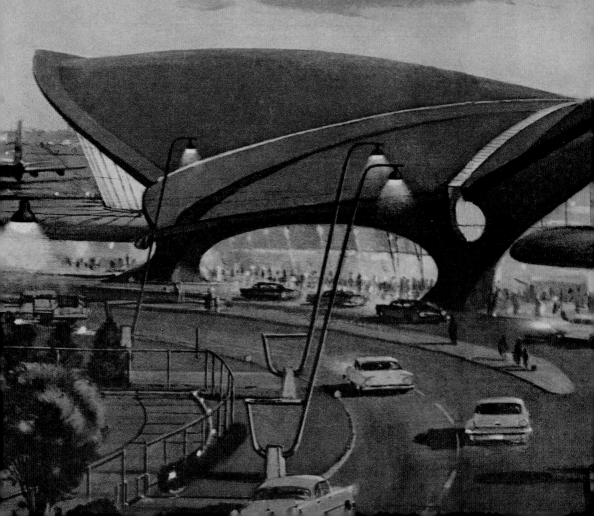

Travel
330

Think of her as your mother.

She only wants what's best for you.
A cool drink. A good dinner. A soft pillow and a warm blanket.
This is not just maternal instinct. It's the result of the longest
Stewardess training in the industry.
Training in service, not just a beauty course.
Service, after all, is what makes professional travellers prefer American.
And makes new travellers want to keep on flying with us.
So we see that every passenger gets the same professional treatment.
That's the American Way.

Fly the American Way
American Airlines

they hate us in New York!

You may wonder how an airline that doesn't go to New York can have enemies there. Well, New Yorkers sometimes travel from, say, Chicago to Los Angeles. Many take our Proud Birds. Frankly, we spoil them, and the next thing you know, they get angry because we don't serve New York.

The reason we spoil them is that our people have an almost patriotic pride in their airline. They do things with an exacting thoroughness that can only come from a great deal of personal pride—and you feel comfortable. Confident.

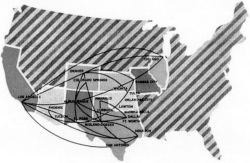

The Continental States of America
Growing with pride

To be sure you know exactly where these good things happen, we've invented a country. We call it the Continental States of America. If you're ever there—come travel with us and feel the difference pride makes. Your travel agent or Continental will arrange it. Please call.

Continental Airlines
the proud bird with the golden tail

Enjoy fine bistro swift at "Good Neighbor Sam," starring Jack Lemmon and Romy Schneider. A David Swift production. A Columbia release.　　　Films by Inflight Motion Pictures, Inc.

Across the U.S., across the Atlantic: **Movies in flight are here　...only on TWA jets!**

EARPHONES are so lightweight and comfortable you'll forget they're on. And while you're listening, no one else will be disturbed.

VOLUME is adjusted by a single, simple control of your fingertips. Then just relax and be entertained by the best from Hollywood and Europe.

DINING is an experience on TWA. First Class meals are elegant feasts. In Jet Coach or Economy, they're not quite as elaborate but certainly as delicious.

*Optional on $1 in Coach and Economy. Complimentary in First Class.

Picture yourself skimming along on a big TWA jet— 600 mph or better, but so smooth and quiet you'd never know it. You put on featherweight earphones, adjust a fingertip volume control, settle back...and watch a movie! Not the one you saw last year, but the one that just hit Broadway. Movies in flight— today's most talked-about airline service, and only Trans World Airlines has it!

The films are shown on non-stop TWA transcontinental flights in First Class, and now in the Coach* section too! On transatlantic flights, in both First Class and Economy.* If you're planning a vacation trip to the World's Fair this year, or maybe a holiday in Europe —see how much more the right airline buys. Call your nearest Trans World Airlines office, or see your travel agent and specify TWA.

Nationwide Worldwide depend on ✈ **TWA**

TWA, 1964

FAST-GROWING TWA HAS JETS, ROUTES, SERVICES FOR EVERY TRAVELER

Jet speed isn't news any more. Crossing the country in 4½ hours, or the Atlantic in 6½ hours, is an everyday fact. And not just for the well-to-do. A department store buyer is likely to be sitting across the aisle from a corporation president. A secretary on a vacation tour shares the same jet with an heiress on a winter holiday. Everybody's flying.

With the big boom in air travel has come a new attitude toward airlines. Most passengers aren't awed by the huge jets and ultra-modern terminals. They're getting more sophisticated about the whole idea of flying, and more perceptive when it comes to buying a ticket. They want to know what one airline has that another hasn't. They're taking a new interest in schedules, performance records, dependability, fares, equipment, personnel. In short, they're asking, "What's in it for me?"

To come up with the right answers, airlines are offering more new services and conveniences than ever before. These pages will show you what fast-growing Trans World Airlines does to stay ahead in the competition for passengers.

Passengers enjoy first-run movies such as the Metro-Goldwyn-Mayer Arts production, "Sunday in New York," starring Cliff Robertson, Jane Fonda and Rod Taylor.

Nationwide Worldwide depend on ✈ **TWA**

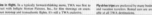

Precision teamwork from flight and ground crews pays off in an excellent record of on-time performance for TWA. The New York Trans World Flight Center in the background, one of many new TWA terminals, houses every passenger convenience.

Movies in flight. In a typically forward-thinking move, TWA was first to contract with Inflight Motion Pictures, Inc., for film showings on coast-to-coast nonstop and transatlantic flights. It's still a TWA exclusive.

Fly-drive trips are preferred by many business and vacation travelers. Rental cars are available at all TWA destinations.

Instant reservations. With TWA's new computer system, a touch of a button confirms a reservation on any flight in less than one second.

Careful attention to service is standard on TWA. Steaks, for instance, come sizzling hot from compact electronic ovens.

Newest jet, the medium-range StarStream 727, needs less runway space, will fly between Chicago, Philadelphia, Pittsburgh and other cities. More long-range StarStreams are also coming soon to beef up what is already the world's largest Boeing jet fleet.

"Family Fun" travel plan offers, for the first time, family discounts on new Jet Coach fares. Full fare for one parent, 25% off for the rest of the family (50% if they're under 12). Same discounts in First Class.

International routes. Only TWA flies from major U.S. cities to New York and the World's Fair—and overseas to 15 world centers.

Fast, accurate information is essential to TWA efficiency. Any change in flight data are flashed instantly to TWA ground hostesses and counter personnel by electronic "Selsvi" flight boards and closed-circuit TV.

United, 1962 ◄　TWA, 1964

THE NEW
707 ★ ASTROJET®

AMERICAN AIRLINES OPENS _JET AGE: STAGE II,_
introducing the world's most advanced, most dependable jetliner in
daily transcontinental passenger service. ■ American's fleet of Astrojets
will bring you a new standard in jet performance by the airline that's
first choice of experienced travelers. ■ The 707 Astrojet easily outper-
forms all other airlines. Its more powerful Jet-Fan engines represent
the most significant advance in commercial aviation since the development of the original jet engine. ■ Powered by these new Jet-Fan engines,
American's 707 Astrojet has the
thrust for quicker take-off, using
far less runway than the best of
standard jets. You'll enjoy a wonderful sense of confidence as you experience the
Astrojet's exceptional rate of climb—as you relax on
the jet that cruises smoothly, easily, within the transonic range at
speeds unsurpassed by any jetliner in the world ■ In keeping with a 25-year
tradition of leadership, American is proud to be first in bringing you this
new dimension in jet travel—this historic new era in air transportation.

AMERICAN AIRLINES
America's Leading Airline

American Airlines, 1961

TWA StarStream Theater. Wide-screen color movies presented
by Inflight Motion Pictures. Plus 8 audio channels, including
popular and classical music in stereo, jazz, musical theater, drama,
comedy, history. Private earphones, individual volume controls.
You won't be disturbed, you won't disturb anybody else. Now on
coast-to-coast jets, soon on jets to Europe.

Continental café. TWA Royal Ambassador First Class offers four
elegant entrees: Stuffed Cornish Hen Veronique, Filet Mignon
broiled to perfection, Lobster Cardinal, Lamb Chops. Make your
selection right on the jet. Cocktails, canapés, champagne, of course,
and still wine. In Coach meals are not as lavish, but the same
care goes into them. The Club Steak is a delicious example.

TWA has the most entertaining ideas in air travel.

There's a whole jetful of easy living for you on TWA. No other airline does
more to make every mile of the way a pleasant, relaxing experience.
What makes the difference on TWA? Quality. Good movies on big screens,
in full color. Entertainment by outstanding artists on Columbia Records and
Epic Records . . . Barbra Streisand, Tony Bennett, Dave Brubeck, Leonard
Bernstein, Richard Burton, dozens more. Superb food, prepared right on the
jet. And people who make the extra effort to make you feel at home.
In short, the best things aboard air travel. And you get them all on one airline.

TWA, 1965

Look what the Russians are building, just 40 miles from the U.S.A.

As an American, you should look into it.

The U.S.S.R. hopes you will. You're invited to step in, and take a look at life in the Soviet Union. Meet the people, see what they do for a living in Vladivostok or Minsk, and how they have fun.

What kind of ideas do the Russians have, about education, medicine, housing, industrial development, space exploration? You'll find out here. In the great Lunar Hall, they'll treat you to an eerie expedition to the moon. On the way, you'll discover what the feeling of weightlessness is like (just *how* is their secret).

And on the lighter side of things, you can see what the Moscow miss is wearing, at a fashion parade. Browse through nearby stores that sell the identical items you'd find in shops in Leningrad or Kiev. Drop into the 600-seat cinema and watch a Russian movie. And wind up in one of

the restaurants, where you can take your pick of specialties from every part of the country. (Incidentally, they've ordered 20 tons of sturgeon, eight tons of caviar and 28,000 litres of vodka, just for starters.)

The place to come for this fascinating experience is the U.S.S.R. Pavilion at Expo 67, Montreal, Canada. It's just across the way from the giant U.S.A. Pavilion — another world of wonders. And a few steps away, the French, British, Italians, Japanese, Canadians — more than two thirds of all the nations on earth — spread before you the best of their arts and culture. The latest in science and technology. Their past, present and future.

In all, some 70 governments have spent hundreds of millions of dollars to make Expo 67 the greatest world exhibition of them all, and the *first of its kind* on this continent. It opens on April 28th, for six wonderful months only. You'll find it the experience of a lifetime.

Start planning now. Expo 67 admission tickets *at reduced advance prices* save you up to 29%, are on sale at banks, department stores, American Express offices, and wherever you see the Expo 67 sign.

Accommodations in Montreal? No need to worry. LOGEXPO, the official accommodation bureau, guarantees you a place to stay, at government controlled prices. Reserve now — just write, mentioning dates, type of accommodations preferred, and the number in your party, to LOGEXPO, Expo 67, Harbor City, Montreal, Quebec, Canada. Or see your travel agent.

Or write for free Expo 67 vacation planning information to Expo 67 Information Services, 150 Kent St., Ottawa, Ont., Canada.

expo67
MONTRÉAL, CANADA
The Universal and International Exhibition of 1967
Montreal, Canada/APRIL 28-OCTOBER 27, 1967
© Copyright, 1963, by the Canadian Corporation for the 1967 World Exhibition

IN LAS VEGAS

NOW 1,000 ROOMS

AT HOTEL

SAHARA

Your Key to a TREASURE OF PLEASURE

Hotel Sahara . . . the new vacation wonder in the world's wonder city . . . now with 1,000 rooms and room for everbody! All the luxurious leisure, the fun and relaxation you expect in one of the world's finest resort hotels...at rates anyone can afford.

Sun-swimming in three spacious pools . . . dining in three famous restaurants...star entertainment in two great showrooms. Shops, buffets, health club, golfing, riding... a real "Treasure of Pleasure"—the vacation visit of a lifetime, Hotel Sahara!

ALSO—THE WEST'S MOST COMPLETE AND LUXURIOUS PRIVATE CONVENTION FACILITIES—FOR 10 TO 1600 PERSONS.

| 1,000 "YEARS-AHEAD" ROOMS all with radio and TV. | DON THE BEACHCOMBER dining-dancing. | HOUSE OF LORDS elegant dining. | THREE LUXURIOUS SWIMPOOLS temperature-controlled. | LIVELY CASBAR THEATRE dusk-'til-dawn shows. |

STAR-STUDDED SHOWS in the great Congo Room, where famous names reign supreme. Colorful, captivating show productions!

HOTEL
SAHARA
LAS VEGAS · NEVADA

Enjoy a "GOLDEN WEB OF HOSPITALITY" at these other DEL E. WEBB hotels: MOUNTAIN SHADOWS · SCOTTSDALE, ARIZ. / OCEAN HOUSE · SAN DIEGO / TOWN HOUSE · SAN FRANCISCO

Expo 67, 1967 ◄ *Sahara, 1963*

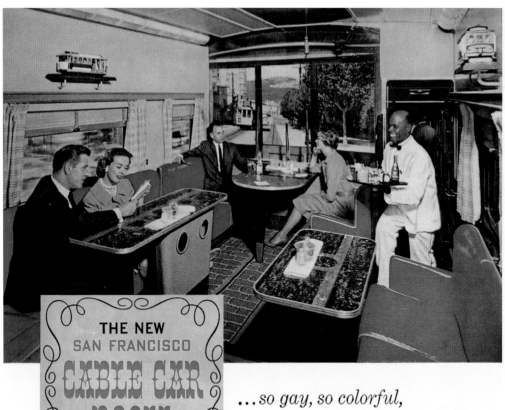

California Zephyr, 1961

Dome dining, an exclusive feature on the Domeliners "City of Los Angeles" and "City of Portland"

Domeliners and Fall...

the nicest travel combination of all!

There's nothing quite like Fall in the Midwest and East for that late vacation or combination business and pleasure trip. ☐ Nature, cloaked in flaming hues, is at her gayest and there's an exhilarating tang in the air that quickens the step and lightens the spirit. Adding to the color and excitement are the 50 yard line views of the colorful countryside from see-level Dome cars, including the only Dome Diner between Los Angeles and Chicago. ☐ Along with the delightful dining and lounge facilities, the modern Coach and Pullman accommodations, you'll find traveling by Domeliner adds to the pleasant memories. ☐ And money-saving Family Fares for husband and wife, as well as families with youngsters, make travel by Domeliner as economical as it is enjoyable!

DOMELINERS "City of Los Angeles" — "The Challenger" to Salt Lake City, Omaha, Chicago
"The City of St. Louis" to Denver, Kansas City, St. Louis

UNION PACIFIC RAILROAD

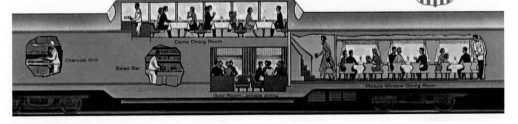

COME
AS YOU
ARE

Star of the Red Skelton Show (CBS–TV, 8:30 p.m. Tuesdays) relaxes in one of the opulent new Penthouse Suites at the Sands

*Come to The Sands Hotel—where even the stars relax. Where the Crowned Heads of the entertainment world deliver incomparable Copa Room performances night after unforgettable night! □ Come to The Sands and see the lavishly appointed new Penthouse Suites. Sample the striking, unique Petite Suites. Relax in magnificently decorated Rooms. And dine amid courtly splendor in the mural-lined new Garden Room. □ Come to The Sands where the gracious Continental hospitality is spiced with the Monte Carlo whirl of excitement 24 hours every thrilling day and night! Where the swimming, the **free golf**, the sightseeing—and even the sun—are superlative! □ Come to The Sands now. Come as you are. A swift, five hours or less by Jet from Anywhere, U.S.A. The Sands is the "Address of Success" in fabulous Las Vegas.*

LET'S JET TO THE **Sands**

LAS VEGAS, NEVADA

COMPLETE CONVENTION FACILITIES *including Private Meeting and Dining Rooms.*
NOW BOOKING FUTURE RESERVATIONS. *Call your Local Travel Agent or our Nearest Office:* Chicago/CEntral 6-3317
Dallas/RIverside 2-6959 ⋅ Las Vegas/REgent 5-9111 ⋅ Los Angeles/BRadshaw 2-8611 ⋅ New York/PLaza 7-4454
Pittsburgh/EXpress 1-4028 ⋅ San Francisco/EXbrook 7-2287 ⋅ Toronto/EMpire 3-6728.

On March 10, Tokyo's legendary hotel begins a new chapter.

In the heart of Tokyo, the Orient's biggest, most luxurious hotel. Fourteen hundred rooms, each with air-conditioning, color television and refrigerator. Ten superb Oriental or Western-cuisine restaurants, including the famous Theatre Restaurant Imperial. An experienced staff of 1,700 ready to assist you in every way. A unique blend of 21st century facilities and 19th century service—in the tradition of luxury begun 80 years ago. The new Imperial . . . and the legend continues. **IMPERIAL HOTEL, TOKYO**

T. Inumaru, President and General Manager

SEATTLE WORLD'S FAIR 1962

It's April 21, 1962, in Seattle...World's Fair time! The curtain's going up on the 21st Century...and on the most exciting preview ever seen. This is Seattle's spectacular Space-Age World's Fair, where the epic of man's journey into the next 100 years will unfold for you. What's ahead? How will man live? What will he see? Look at cities in the year 2000, see homes whose walls are jets of air, where cordless appliances work for you, cars ride without wheels, TV wrist telephones speed everyday communications. Time and distance will disappear in the gigantic, pillar-less Coliseum Century 21, jutting eleven stories up from the heart of the fair. You'll soar past the moon into outer galaxies—no space suit, no gravity, in the $9 million complex of the United States Science Pavilion. You will discover the secrets of the future in these six gleaming buildings rising above lighted fountains and courtyard pools. But it's not all the story of man's great tomorrows. Much of this $80 million show will be a glittering world of today. Dine atop the towering 60-story Space Needle which revolves to view Mt. Rainier, the Olympic and Cascade Ranges. Stroll Boulevards of the World filled with the sights and sounds of foreign lands. Thrill to the Monorail as it whisks you the mile from downtown Seattle in 95 seconds.

Rembrandt, Gauguin, and 65 world masters have been specially loaned for the Fair

Cultures of foreign lands in a potpourri of color and fun in the Boulevards of the World

Enjoy famed artists from all over the world performing in the opulent Opera House, intimate Playhouse, the Arena and Stadium. Relax in a rollicking Gayway where special rides hold fun-appeal to all ages. The Seattle World's Fair...the big family adventure of our times! See it all, April 21 to October 21, in Seattle!

Washington State Department of Commerce & Economic Development, Albert D. Rosellini, Governor.

SEATTLE WORLD'S FAIR, SEATTLE 9, WASH.

Please send me the following:

Further information about a Washington State vacation ☐

Further information about Seattle World's Fair ☐

Further information about housing accommodations ☐

WASHINGTON is a Thrill-Filled State ...See It All While You're Here!

NAME _____

ADDRESS _____

CITY _____ STATE _____

(PLEASE PRINT CLEARLY)   C-21 LN

OPENS APRIL 21

SEATTLE WORLD'S FAIR 1962

The curtain's going up on America's first World's Fair in two decades. For 180 days, millions will step beyond the boundaries of today's world for a way-ahead look into another age. See for yourself how the family of tomorrow will live, work and play in the most spectacular, breathtaking forecast science ever made. Preview out-of-this-world concepts of living in space . . . on the ground . . . under the sea! Match it all with the best of our world today—its art, its entertainment, its varied culture—coming to life before your eyes in a sparkling $80 million showcase of pleasure and delight!

A FLOATING CITY OF TOMORROW! A rotating "bubbleator" in Washington State's gigantic Coliseum elevates 100 persons at a time to a fascinating portrayal of life's wonders in the year 2000.

MILE-A-MINUTE MONORAIL! The thrilling ride of a lifetime on the noiseless monorail gliding above busy downtown Seattle streets to its World's Fair terminal . . . 10,000 passengers hourly!

A RESTAURANT THAT REVOLVES IN THE SKY! 600 feet up, the lacy fingers of the Space Needle reach toward the clouds, crowned by an observation deck, dining room, and a soaring jet of flame!

ROCKET RIDE TO MARS! Leave the world behind as you take a just-pretend journey 2 billion light years into space in the Boeing Company's Spacearium at the breath-taking U. S. Science Pavilion.

WORLD'S GREATEST STARS! Stravinsky, The Old Vic, Count Basie: A continuous parade of leading entertainers performs for you in the opulent Opera House, the Playhouse, the Arena and the Stadium.

SHOW STREET! Gorgeous girls take you behind the scenes as part of the act at "Backstage, U. S. A." It's one of the Fair's many glamorous nighteries.

GAY, EXOTIC BOULEVARDS OF THE WORLD! A potpourri of scents, sounds, and tastes from 35 foreign nations. Trees and fountains line the beautifully landscaped malls and plazas.

IT'S A HUGE, GLAMOROUS, EXCITING SHOW set in one of the world's most beautiful modern cities. See it all, starting April 21, for 180 unforgettable days and nights! It's the blazing, amazing adventure of a lifetime . . . the world's salute to a new age!

PACIFIC NORTHWEST OPENS ITS DOORS! A Western welcome and room for all awaits you. For reservations in Washington, Oregon and British Columbia as you travel to and from the Fair—and for your Seattle stay—write Expo-Lodging Service, Inc., Seattle 9, Wash. Confirmed reservations possible in Seattle through Expo-Lodging in hotels, motels, apartment-hotels and approved private homes.

EVERY PLACE YOU WANT TO GO—all the things you want to see . . . are just hours away from the big Seattle show. Take time to see it all. You'll love every minute of it!

WASHINGTON STATE DEPARTMENT OF COMMERCE AND ECONOMIC DEVELOPMENT, Albert D. Rosellini, Governor

Imperial Hotel, 1969 ◄◄ *Seattle World's Fair, 1962* ◄

Seattle World's Fair, 1962

Index